How To Take Back Control Of

The  7 Most

Important Areas Of Your Life

Dr. Erwin Jay, O.D.

Certified Master Practitioner of Neuro-Linguistic Programming

Copyright © 2004 by Erwin Jay, O. D.

ISBN 978-0-7414-1924-8

Published by:

INFINITY
PUBLISHING.COM

1094 New DeHaven Street, Suite 100
West Conshohocken, PA 19428-2713
Info@buybooksontheweb.com
www.buybooksontheweb.com
Toll-free (877) BUY BOOK
Local Phone (610) 941-9999
Fax (610) 941-9959

Printed in the United States of America

Published April 2013

Disclaimer

Acknowledgments

This book would not have been possible without my family and friends, all the countless authors and coaches, fellow associates and patients in my practice over so many years, the inspirational messages from all of the people listed in the references section and all those who are not, but whose impact was and still is very significant.

Starting with my immediate family, my mother convinced her three sons to read a book a week by taking us to the public library on Saturday mornings for the "Story Lady". We would then each take home a book and finish it before the following Saturday. What a great beginning! Dad taught us all about love and caring. They were married for 52 years before he passed on.

Earl Nightingale triggered my first major breakthrough after I graduated from college (see Chapter 1). The rest of you know who you are and I send countless thanks. The latest on my list of favorites is the person who put this text together on the computer and trimmed away anything not needed so that this book is an easy read.

Much Love to Everyone!

Table of Contents

FOREWORD

The purpose of this book is to help you discover more ways to have greater joy in your life on a daily basis and, ultimately, to facilitate a major shift from your current experiences to a state of bliss.

The teachers from ancient India tell us that bliss is the normal state. After studying and teaching human behavior for more than three decades, it is my conclusion that one of the key factors to joyful living with good mental health and physical well-being is a sense of personal control.

Picture yourself driving your car in the late afternoon on your way home from work. The temperature is 25 degrees Fahrenheit, and wet snow is beginning to fall. The highway that leads to your home passes over a bridge, and you spot a customary sign now having more significance than usual. It warns "Bridge Freezes Before Roadway." Whoa! You gently press on the brake pedal to check the traction. Without warning, your car suddenly changes direction, both skidding and starting to spin sideways. Your car is out of control.

Fortunately, there are no other cars in your immediate vicinity while you turn your steering wheel into the skid and return your car to its proper heading. "Whew! That was scary," you say to yourself. You have just experienced first-hand the fear and panic of being temporarily out of control. It has been my experience and observation that extensive fear or panic can produce emotional illness or, at the very least, force us to "travel more cautiously on the 'highway of life' even when the road is dry."

Almost everyone who has driven a car for a lot of years has had one or more out of control experiences similar to the one just described. These experiences personally demonstrate the sense of panic felt when knowing you have no control. In the larger arena of life, our risk of losing our sense of control over one or more areas of daily living increases in direct proportion to the rate of change in our lives. And there is no denying that the pace of change continues to accelerate.

Today we live in an "information age." Historians tell us that it took 75 years, from 1850 to 1925, for the amount of printed information in the world to double. More recently, statisticians say that the doubling of information only takes between five and eight years, or less.

When I graduated from college, a degree was supposed to last a lifetime. Now in the twenty-first century, life-long learning is the rule, with career changes occurring more often than job changes did in the past. Many of my friends are in entirely different careers than what they started after high school, or trained for in college.

Imagine working for a company for twenty years, and you do excellent work. You receive occasional promotions and pay raises. As a result, you feel very comfortable and secure.

One day you pick up a Wall Street Journal and notice a small paragraph stating that a huge conglomerate has offered a bid to acquire the company that you have been working for. You show the information to your immediate supervisor, and she admits to having heard a "rumor" and reassures you that, "This kind of article appears all the time."

Two months later the deal is done, and you have been downsized (a polite way of saying you have been fired), through no fault of your own. Chances are you have bills and dependants, and you feel the loss of any semblance of financial control over your life. Welcome to the growing crowd.

In spite of countless stories like this, we all know some people who simply stand up, dust themselves off, and start all over again. Even more puzzling, these same people seem to be living life to the fullest, getting so much more excitement, fun, and joy out of every passing day. How do they do it? Is there a secret?

The way that many of these individuals take back control of their lives will be shared with you in the pages that follow, along with specific methods that you can apply to your own circumstances. As for any "secret," part of that lies in learning how to acquire a sense of personal control over the most important areas of your life. This book will show you how.

INTRODUCTION

From early childhood I have had an insatiable curiosity about how and why things work the way they do. By the time I was ten years old I was designing, building and flying model airplanes and competing in contests. Years later, I graduated college with a lot of background in medicine, optics, physics, chemistry, and psychology. The one subject that I found most fascinating was psychology and the working of the human mind.

Today, if you watch late night television, you will see ads from drug and pharmaceutical companies appealing directly to consumers, advising them to tell their doctors which drugs they should take, to cure a variety of emotional illnesses. Not too long ago a patient would go to their doctor, discuss their symptoms, perhaps have some tests done and then the DOCTOR would prescribe the course of treatment.

After studying "emotional illness" which some authors describe as illnesses which have no way of proving exist within the body via tests, no verifiable pathology, I have arrived at some conclusions. It is my personal opinion that a lot of these conditions which are very real to the patients, begin with a sense of loss of control over the major events taking place in their lives (see the back cover for a list).

As I mentioned in the disclaimer, this book is in no way designed to diagnose or treat disease. You need to see your M.D. for that. What it can do and will do for you is to help you get very clear on which areas of your life you can regain a sense of control. It has been my observation that people who feel in charge of their lives have fewer challenges that push them into the category of helpless victim. By reading this book and taking action there is a very good chance you can and will acquire methods for dealing more effectively with the challenges most human beings encounter in a lifetime. You have nothing to lose (except some old behaviors you no longer want) and you have everything to gain.

The activities in which we all participate can be classified into two major categories: PROCESS and CONTENT. Imagine pushing a shopping cart in a huge supermarket. Moving the cart up and down the various aisles while viewing the countless items on display is the PROCESS. What you select and put into the cart is the CONTENT. This book focuses on *five major categories of content* and the *related processes* that will help you take back control of your life.

People have many different life goals, or destinations, and despite their best efforts, unfortunately, many of them get off track. I have found that it is often the little difference in the beginning of a process that makes a big difference in the outcome. For instance, if a jet airliner flies out of Los Angeles heading east, the course angle to a destination in New York or Miami is relatively small at the point of departure, but these cities are actually about thirteen hundred miles apart on a map. By making continual flight adjustments, the pilot will determine if the airliner lands in New York, New York, rather than Miami, Florida. Using the ideas in the pages that follow, you will be able to select the correct headings on your journey to your destination, or goal.

When you are in the "supermarket of life," what you put into your shopping cart will determine to a large extent the kind of joy you will get to experience on your journey through life. The various checkpoints and destinations along the way will be determined by the course you select, just as navigators know that reaching their desired destination requires continuous correction to maintain a particular heading.

All of our lives have CONTENT. That might mean having: mothers, fathers, children, siblings, houses, cars, jobs, friends, books, movies, games, food, etc. The one thing we all have, however, is a brain.

The human brain has often been compared to a super-computer. The major difference is that human brains are delivered without an operating manual or "Help" files. This is one of the reasons why we each develop a unique hierarchy, or list of priorities, for our own story. It is this personal order of priorities that greatly influences our individual outcomes.

Once our basic needs are satisfied, we become interested in activities that lead to a feeling of fulfillment, and a sense of purpose or an awareness that life matters. Psychological studies proved that most of our activities occur because we want to change our state, the way we feel at any given moment. If we are tired, we go to sleep. If we are hungry, we eat to get rid of the feeling of hunger and derive the sense of pleasure associated with eating.

Of the seven most important areas of your life, the one that drives the rest is the **DESIRED OUTCOME**. We live in a "results-oriented" society.

So often we confuse "means" values with "ends" values. How to become crystal clear on your desired outcome, the true "ends" values, will unfold as you read what follows.

Most of us go to work to obtain the necessary money to support the life style we desire. Yet, so often, we feel like victims or puppets of "the system," meaning that someone else is in control of our futures even though we live in a country whose promise is freedom of choice, life, liberty, and the pursuit of happiness. Why does success by any definition come to so few?

Let's find out.

CHAPTER ONE

The Earl Nightingale Story

In Zen an "Aha!" experience is called a "*satori.*" We have all seen a cartoon illustration with a light bulb flashing above a person's head indicating a breakthrough experience or idea. My first major *satori* occurred a few years after I graduated from college. I had a degree and was licensed to practice optometry. I had what Zorba (as in "Zorba the Greek") described as "the full catastrophe": a wife, kids, mortgage, and a dog. I also had a new car, and I could not pay for any of it.

Upon graduation I had purchased an optometry practice in a retail location in the inner city. It was failing and I was going broke. A friend of mine knew of my predicament and in an effort to help, offered to take me to hear a live presentation by a motivational speaker. My friend even paid for the ticket because he knew I had no money to spare.

That night was a *satori*, a major turning point in my career. The speaker was Earl Nightingale, known at that time as "The Dean of Motivation." He had a syndicated radio show that was heard on 1100 radio stations coast to coast. Earl and his partner, Lloyd Conant, founded the Nightingale-Conant Corporation which is still in business today and one of the largest producers of motivational tapes and CD's on a wide variety of self-help topics. (I later got to know Earl and Lloyd personally and for five years sponsored their radio show in my home town of Cleveland, Ohio, as a token of appreciation for the help I received that one night.)

The title of Earl's presentation that night was "The Strangest Secret," since heard by several million people. When publicly released, in the now antiquated record form, it became the largest selling non-musical recording ever sold. The program has since been revised, expanded, and updated, and is still available from N.C. Corp. in both cassette and CD. (See the List of References.)

At the risk of over-simplification, on that evening I focused my attention on two key points that changed my life for the better almost overnight. Earl listed these points as *factors*.

I recalled his *first factor* "We become what we think about [most of the time]." Immediately, this familiar quote came to mind, "As a man thinketh, so he becomes."

The *second factor* was "the danger of conformity." This really hit a nerve in me. In college I was forced to conform if I wanted to receive passing grades. In short, the teacher taught and you memorized. There was no room for independent thinking in the pre-med or optometry classes. We studied the "Laws of Physics and Optics," and were reminded ad nauseum via our instructors that: "The laws of physics have never been repealed. Learn them well."

When I graduated, I did what almost everybody in my class did. I found a practice owned by an older doctor and went to work. When he retired, I bought the practice. What I did not recognize at the time was the fact that, like the doctor, the practice also had a terminal illness.

My college days were so filled with technical information and college clinical experience that there was no room for business courses to prepare me to run the financial end of my practice. I later discovered that many of my classmates were also in financial difficulty, going through what was classified as the "starvation period" of building, or rebuilding, a practice. This period was acceptable to most. In fact, many graduates went back to their hometowns to live with parents in order to keep overhead expenses low, while they tried to build a practice.

When I heard Earl explain the danger of conformity, he said,

> Out of 100 people starting out from age 21 and followed to age 65, only ONE will be so rich that he or she can buy anything they want without worrying about the cost. Another three or four will have income from investments adequate to be financially independent, but usually at a lower standard of living than one they enjoyed while working. The rest will either be dead or dead broke.

Today, the numbers are a little better, due to pension plans, stock options, and tax shelters. The real success stories, however, are still a very small percentage of the total. Unfortunately, the downsizing of corporate America is challenging even these small numbers.

Earl went on to explain that statistics showed that only five out of 100 people actually succeed financially in the United States, the richest major country in the world. If you pattern yourself after just anybody, the odds are 19:1 AGAINST success, since 95 out of 100 do NOT succeed.

That's when the light went on for me.

When I simply went out and, like my classmates, bought another's practice I had conformed to the masses, instead of carefully seeking out a truly successful role model. I felt like Earl was talking just to me and miraculously, on this night the remedy, the solution, became obvious to me.

1. Find someone who is not only doing what you want to do, but what is a hundred times more important, GETTING THE KIND OF RESULTS, THE OUTCOME, THAT YOU DESIRE.

2. Find out HOW THEY DO WHAT THEY DO, SPECIFICALLY! The more specific you are, the better are your chances for duplicating their successes.

3. Acquire the necessary skills, equipment, etc.

4. DO THE SAME THINGS THEY DO!

5. You will, with persistence, get the same or very similar RESULTS.

At first this seemed too simple, too good to be true. My doubting, scientific nature said there has to be a "catch" somewhere. (There is. It is called human inertia, or resistance to change. I will have more on this in a later chapter.)

Later, when I got to know Earl personally, I asked, "How did you come up with the title, 'The Strangest Secret'?" He explained:

> I have been traveling across the country giving this message to thousands of people, and many thousands have purchased the recording. Yet, even among those who attend my lectures, or

hear the recordings, the number of successful people does not seem to change significantly. I find that very strange. It is as if someone handed you a guaranteed map showing buried treasure that could make you rich and give you all the money you will ever need right in your own backyard, but you elected to not bother and dig it up. After all, digging is hard work. Personally, I think being poor is harder than digging, although it certainly requires less effort. So, I think that is strange.

As for the use of SECRET, if I share this important message with literally thousands of people who pay good money to hear it and then they go home and do not utilize even one good idea, it might as well BE SECRET, at least to them. It is like having an excellent book that contains marvelous recipes for baking bread, but instead you keep trying to do it without any recipe and only succeed in wasting ingredients and making a mess, but no bread. Then you complain because you are hungry or have bad luck. So, I call it 'The Strangest Secret'.

I got it!

So why is it that people say they want to change, but resist the change? Part of it has to do with their self-image. Dr. Maxwell Maltz, author of one of the first self-image psychology books, <u>Psycho-Cybernetics</u>[*] stated, "Everything we do, must, of necessity, be consistent with our own self-image." One of the things that holds people back from more fully realizing their own potential is their own concept of self-worth,

---

[*] see references

usually formulated before the age of reason, under the guidance of well-intentioned, but poorly trained parents. Like our brains, children also come without an operations manual.

Well-intentioned parents want their children to survive. However, where do the parents usually acquire parenting skills? Answer: From their own amateur parents.

Sometimes we do not realize that the things our parent's told us when we were children still direct, at an unconscious level, our present behaviors. To understand this let's look at another field of psychology called Transactional Analysis, abbreviated T.A. In this training, the example of patterns of behavior is described in three *ego states*: Parent, Adult, and Child; capitalized to differentiate from the other usage of the words.

The *Parent ego state* acts like an instant replay cassette recorder, using phrases much like your parents did, "Don't touch the stove, it's hot," or "Look both ways before you cross the street," and a host of other survival suggestions or injunctions. Since a young child is virtually dependent on their parents, almost everything they hear from authority figures is believed to be an absolute truth.

Many of these perceived "survival skills" are received by a child before he/she reaches the age of reason. These children, armed only with this data from many well-intentioned but uninformed parents, are at the same time also hearing phrases like, "Be careful, you are so clumsy." or, "You *always* make a mess of things" or, "You are *always* doing such stupid things." or, "You are worthless, such a baby, etc."

Once a child *"buys in"* to these labels, he or she will, from that point in time, always think of themselves as lazy, clumsy, or stupid and, unfortunately, these are the concepts that help to form a negative or low self-image. Think of some of the negative things you heard as a child growing up. Make a list. Now pause and ask yourself, "Do I still think of myself that way?"

Is it possible to change our self-image? The answer is *yes*. Psycho-Cybernetics by Dr. Maxwell Maltz and other more recent books by Dr. Nathaniel Branden are excellent resources for acquiring these skills, so I will not go into great detail here. But, remember this important fact, again: "Everything we do (especially if it can have major consequences) *must*, of necessity, be consistent with our own self-image." Fortunately, self-images can be changed for the better with a little guided practice. This is why so many authors have written, "Fake it 'til you make it." In other words, *look, think*, and *act* as if you were already the kind of person you want to become.

This *visualization* technique has worked for many people. It works best if past beliefs are examined along with present-age adult beliefs to see if any still do (or ever did) apply. For example, perhaps you were a somewhat clumsy child, but outgrew those tendencies. Consider what is now more important, those former beliefs or your present abilities? For any beliefs or characteristics from the past, techniques covered in this text or listed in the references will show you how to "grow up the part" so that former inappropriate beliefs are no longer seen in that way.

As a child growing up, I was over-weight. My father was in the wholesale food business and sold butter, eggs and cheese to grocery stores. (How is that for a cholesterol send-off?)

At that time period, FAT was synonymous with HEALTHY. "Look at him; he is such a FAT, HEALTHY baby." Getting past that one took me more than twenty-five years and a dangerous increase in blood pressure before I re-examined it in the light of current medical knowledge.

Another "brilliant" parenting technique (which I blame to this day for a lot of the overweight population) is using dessert or sweets as a reward for good behavior. "Finish your plate and THEN you can have dessert."

What rocket scientist concluded that the way to good health is to cram in a 1200 calorie meal so you will then be ENTITLED to reward yourself with another 600 or 800 additional calories on top of the meal? Then we wonder why overweight people, who feel bad enough, will eat desserts to feel better, if only for a short while. In most cases they learned this from well-intentioned parents. Just visit any all-you-can-eat buffet, and see the type of people they attract. Then be sympathetic and realize that many of them are being governed by unexamined early childhood beliefs.

Do they have other choices? Sure, once they can understand that this behavior is inconsistent with the desired outcome and that there are forms of behavior modification that can be much more effective than most diet plans. Usually, they include finding healthier ways to make yourself feel good, without using unhealthy fat-filled sweets. This is one of the reasons why it appears that half of the products in the grocery's shelves are labeled low-fat or lean. However, you still have to read the labels to determine fat and sugar content for yourself.

Now, thirty years later, it is still the same. We live in a time period described as the information age. Yet, less than five percent of the total population buys and reads one or more non-fiction or self-help books per year. Some estimates indicate only three percent of us own and use library cards.

Of course, we have other sources of information: radio, TV's "Discovery Channel", PBS and the Internet. Yet, how many evenings have you been disappointed because you could not find anything on TV worth staying up to watch?

For me, a good book is like a good friend who is willing to share their lifetime of experience with me. A book condenses into two or three hours the *extract*, or the real essence, of the author's expertise. Lloyd Conant used to show a picture of an old-fashioned winepress to his friends. He said, "It takes a lot of grapes and much patience to make wine, but you get the essence, the extract, and a good book is just like that."

It may take the writer many years to compile the data. He or she has to live the experience both good and bad, the successes and the failures (now called feedback or learning experiences). They must convey all of the sights, sounds and feelings, even aromas and tastes with word descriptions that can make you laugh or cry, imagine all kinds of pictures and even recall smells and tastes.

You can do this in a miniscule fraction of the time it takes the author to experience and acquire the knowledge of the best experts in any field of endeavor, perhaps thirty years of work condensed into a few hours. With the printed page, the book becomes a reference. Each reading offers additional insights and eliminates the need to be memorized at a single pass.

Let me share with you my own change of fortune that I attribute in large part to hearing "The Strangest Secret." When I tried to thank Earl personally, he reminded me modestly, "When the student is ready, the teacher will appear."

Well, I must have been very ready and he was a marvelous teacher. Since that time many other teachers have appeared when I was ready and I have become a professional student who is also a teacher to others.

By listening to Earl and studying other leading experts in the field, I was able to look at my past, realize the parts that were not working or that were holding me back, and CHOOSE to follow the leaders to do what they do instead. Here is how and what fully implementing the lessons in "The Strangest Secret" did for me. I use this solely as an example based on my own personal experience. I know this is factual, not Pollyanna, because it happened to me.

Within a few days of hearing the message for the first time, I realized that unless I made some major changes immediately, I would not succeed financially in my chosen profession and would have virtually wasted all of the years in college. I do know that a college education is intended to do more than help you earn a living. All of the liberal arts, philosophy, psychology, literature and other studies can and do lead to a greater sense of appreciation for everything in life.

But we do have a hierarchy of needs and wants. When you do not have enough money for food, the only literature that comes to mind is "To be or not to be...," as in alive, hungry and broke, or able to pay the bills.

Summing up all the courage I had from my new knowledge and utilizing all of the sales skills I acquired in college selling Fuller brushes door-to-door one year and encyclopedias another (great training), I went to every relative I could and borrowed enough money to do what Earl said to do.

First, I wrote or called the leading publications in the field of eye care and obtained the names, addresses and phone numbers of the top five optometrists that the editors thought had the largest, most successful practices in the United States. I then confirmed this list with another one from the national sales representatives from manufacturers of contact lenses and eyeglass frames. I figured that they knew who their best customers were.

To get this information, I briefly described my plan and added, "When I have as big a practice as the leaders, I too will be one of your biggest and best customers." Then I crisscrossed the lists from the editors and the manufacturers and selected the top five. This was followed by writing an individual letter to each of them, asking for permission to come and spend a full day with each one to see their offices in action.

I qualified my letter because I wanted to eliminate any fear or reservations they might have. First, I stated that I did not have a license to practice in their state (each state had individual licensing requirements) so I could not be competition to them once I learned their success secrets. Then, I stated that my research indicated that they had one of the top five practices in this country, whereas my own practice was in deep trouble, and I was going broke and on the verge of quitting Optometry.

I mentioned hearing a speaker whose message was to use the ideas that winners do. So, I needed to find out what thing or things they did that set them apart. Why were they so far above the averages?

Today, we call this *modeling excellence*. Tom Peters, author of <u>In Search of Excellence</u>[*] and others have written numerous books on this subject and the entire field of NLP teaches how to do this most efficiently and most effectively. The results were miraculous. Today I believe in miracles, but back then I was truly amazed at the events that followed.

First, every single one wrote or called almost immediately and said, "Do not quit, I will show you how to be successful!" We worked out the dates, one by one.

I got picked up at the airport. I was wined and dined; as their guest, I was not allowed by anybody to pick up a check at a restaurant. Two of them invited me to sleep overnight in their homes to save me the cost of a hotel room and so we would have more time to talk late into the evening and early in the morning. I was in a daze!

When I visited each office, the story was the same. They showed me their books, confidential income and expenses records, earning statements and income tax returns. I could not believe that I, a total stranger, could be treated this way. But these leaders were so successful they wanted to share, to motivate me to succeed. After all, I was a colleague, a fellow eye care

---

[*] see references

professional, like a fraternity brother who was temporarily down on his luck and needing a boost.

I will never forget the new-found joy. I KNEW everything was going to be all right. I had the magic formulas, the recipes. All I had to do was to repeat the same things they did in the same way. One thing they all had in common was some form of specialty. (Specialists usually make more than general practitioners.)

When I returned, I convinced an older, more successful optometrist friend of mine to become my financial mentor in order to open up a new contact lens practice. I spent countless hours becoming extremely proficient, visiting manufacturers so I could literally make my own lenses. I visited the top contact lens fitters (with more borrowed money) with results identical to my earlier trip. They taught me how to rapidly build a successful practice. I formed a partnership with my mentor. I would do all of the work and he would put up the money for a 50/50 partnership. He had the better deal, but he also had the money I needed to start the practice and I did not.

Within one year we made enough for me to draw a salary and repay his entire loan. Within five years we had the second largest contact lens practice in our city and within five more years we were doing TEN TIMES the volume of the average successful practice!

Since that time I have discovered that this is true in most industries or businesses. The top five percent of the businesses do several MULTIPLES of the average, five, ten, or twenty TIMES better, not just a small percentage.

In magazines like Forbes, Success, Selling, and Boardroom Reports, every month you can study dozens of success stories in a wide variety of fields. A visit to a library reference section reveals a gold mine of "How I did it" stories.

Most industries have trade shows and conventions where you can meet the leaders in person and ask your questions or set up an appointment to come and visit them. I know this works because I have done it in several fields. The method works, to the extent that you are willing to implement it. I am repeating it again, because it is so important.

I. We become what we think about most of the time. Affirmations DO work, if they are followed with a plan and action.

II. The Danger of Conformity. The odds are 19 to 1 against success UNLESS you carefully conform to a leader, one of the top 5%.

1. Determine in advance, what is your desired outcome? What do you want?

2. Find someone who has already obtained the kind of results you want.

3. Find out as much as you can about HOW they did it, the little differences in the beginning that make the BIG difference in the outcome.

4. Write your plan of action. There is hidden power in the plan that is written, versus an "idea" we have for our "someday-file," which seldom materializes.

5. Implement the Plan. The best plans do require action and implementation.

Here is an interesting observation. Another quote from Earl is that "Successful people do the things that failures do not like to do." However, it took me many years to discover that successful people DO NOT LIKE DOING THEM EITHER. But, they do them ANYHOW, because they KNOW the importance.

We know, for example, that physical fitness is a daily job, not occasional. One does not acquire the body-build of an Arnold Schwarzenegger by working out just once a week at the local health club.

A very successful star of movies and a television series said, "Successful people in any field know that you have to pay dues to remain successful!" Whether it is cold calling or mail correspondence, business travel to see clients, reading all the current literature in your field, you just do it, if you want to be successful.

As I mentioned before, in the same respect, a farmer knows that you must plant in the spring to have a harvest in the fall. H.L. Hunt, one of the wealthiest men in the country said, "Everything has a price, pay the price UP FRONT. Then you can really enjoy what you bought." Too many people are in a hurry to get something for nothing in life. They want the benefit first before they are willing to put forth the effort. But there really isn't such a thing as something for nothing. Everything worth having has a price.

These responsibilities will be easier to fulfill if you are engaged in a labor of love. Choice of career becomes extremely essential. Do you love what you do on a daily basis? If not, is there some thing you could do that would be a labor of love that would bring you the kind of results you desire? Until you can define and materialize that, find the parts of your present work that are the most enjoyable. Then, do the least enjoyable parts first. Get them done and out of the way, as early on in the day as you can, so you can then be free to spend the rest of the time on the more enjoyable tasks and end your work day on a positive note.

The tendency for less successful people is to put off these unpleasant parts until last. This ends the day in a negative fashion and adversely impacts your home life, your evenings, your eating of the evening meal and even your sleep patterns. Try reversing this habit and notice the positive difference it makes. Get the unpleasant tasks out of the way *first*.

For example, people who exercise on a regular basis, and physical fitness personal trainers, will tell you that those who exercise in the morning tend to remain on their programs much longer and on a more regular basis than those who try to exercise in the evening. It seems that there are more distractions in the evening hours and so many other social functions that vie for your time after the day's work is completed.

For many people, energy levels tend to be highest earlier in the day. If you have some required tasks to complete that are lower on the "fun scale," try to get them finished as early in the day as possible. Tasks that are fun to do tend to provide their own energy later in the day. We have all been engaged in some exciting work where we literally lose track of time. This is one of the eight factors of FLOW* experiences. When you are in the state of flow, energy is not a problem. To learn more about this, read <u>Finding Flow</u>*1 by Mihaly Csikszentmihali.

By finishing each day on a positive note, your evenings are always more rewarding in many ways. This fact makes it worth doing the less pleasant tasks earlier in the day, whenever possible. If you have been in the habit of doing it the other way, try this method for just one week. You will never go back to the old way.

---

[1] see references

CHAPTER TWO

The Five Categories of Content

Anthony Robbins, author and star of the all-time best-selling television infomercials, claimed that he discovered one of the keys to his success through the study of Neuro-Linguistic Programming (NLP), a field that teaches the art and science of modeling excellence. His realization of the importance of modeling excellence parallels my own beliefs, which I had already adopted twenty years before NLP was formalized by its originators Richard Bandler and John Grinder. It was through a serendipitous invitation to hear a live presentation by the motivational speaker Earl Nightingale that I learned and felt the influence of "modeling excellence," as I explained in Chapter 1.

My own research into the field of NLP concurs with that of many experts, particularly regarding the areas of CONTENT we each find important. Naturally, human beings want to simplify any system of organization, and one convenient method is to limit the number of categories or areas of investigation. One author may suggest "seven rules," another "twelve keys to success," and yet another "six magic words." When I look at any of these "recipes" or "formulas" for success, I want to know - *What kinds of results are produced?*

In order to answer this question, I have come to believe that CONTENT can be conveniently studied, if five major categories are utilized and (equally important) our personal priorities are taken into consideration. I have divided CONTENT into these five categories:

- KNOWING
- BEING
- DOING
- GETTING and HAVING
- RELATIONSHIPS

If you listen attentively to any personal conversation for an extended length of time, several things will become apparent. First, *everyone will have some interests in each category.* Secondly, *people attach a different level of importance to each category to develop their own order of hierarchy or priority.*

In the following quotes, notice the connection to each particular *category:*

- KNOWING

"There's a new book about computers. I can't wait to read it because I can learn about the latest technology."

- BEING

"When I grow up, I want to be a movie star."

- DOING

"I see T-shirts with the logo 'JUST DO IT' ™ at every sporting event."

- GETTING and HAVING

"I'm on my way to pick up my new car. My neighbors will really be surprised."

- RELATIONSHIPS

"My whole family is coming to stay for the holidays. We're going to have a great time!"

Have you ever noticed the custom frames many people put around their auto license plates? They give clues to the *level of importance* a person has placed on these categories of CONTENT.

For instance, here are a few that I have seen in my home state of Ohio. Can you guess what CONTENT category is at the top of these car owners' lists?

- "Happiness is being a grandparent."
- "My other car is an airplane."
- "I'd rather be FISHING [or FLYING or BOATING or SAILING or SKYDIVING, etc.]."
- "RETIRED. No phone, no home, no bills, no money."

Let me give you an example of *levels of importance* from another area of investigation to use as an additional basis for comparison:

When interviewing a new job applicant, personnel in Human Resources (formerly referred to as a personnel office or department), will often use psychological assessments to determine a "personality profile" to determine the match of the applicant to a specific job. The hope is to forecast or predetermine each applicant's chances for succeeding on the new job. This reduces turnover and the associated expenses of training the wrong applicant.

Studies show that when candidates are asked questions about "life values," (What is important to you?) three priorities show up most frequently: health, career, and family. At first glance we could conclude that anyone listing these as the top three on their list would probably be a good applicant and have similar job performance. Yet, these three listings can create six possible combinations:

1. health, career, family
2. health, family, career
3. career, family, health
4. career, health, family
5. family, health, career
6. family, career, health

Think about it. The individual who puts career first is going to have different *levels of importance*, or value system, than the others. Moving the family to follow a job is a given. However, for the person that lists family first, the chances are they will pass up the promotion if it means relocating. They may not want to disrupt the continuity in their children's educational, social, or emotional lives, especially if the new location offers less than ideal conditions. They may also want to stay within close proximity to aging parents or the support system of their extended family.

For the person whose health comes first, the issue may not be relocation, but the ability to mentally leave their job at the office, and not having to work unconventional hours or overtime. These factors could interfere with their physical fitness program or sports-related recreational activities, as well as the time it takes to eat scheduled nutritional meals and get adequate sleep.

If you have had similar challenges, can you recall how you felt at decision time? Obviously, within the CONTENT of your list, you must not only consider *all the categories,* but you must also take into consideration the *level of importance* of each.

Dr. Abraham Maslow is best known for his work on the human hierarchy of needs. Let's review one of his excellent works. You can get an audiotape on "Self Actualization"* for greater detail.

Briefly, Maslow demonstrated his ideas on the hierarchy of human needs in the form of a pyramid. He believed that until you satisfy the basic or lower levels it is extremely difficult, if not impossible, to rise to the next level. You have to start at the bottom and work your way up, one level at a time.

Knowing this helps to understand why we sometimes make plans and then fail to execute them. If I am very hungry because I skipped a meal and my schedule says that I am supposed to go to the gym to exercise, I might stop to eat on the way and then chances are after I eat that I might not feel like working out.

Once I recall the hierarchy I can wait a short while for the food to digest and then exercise or I can tell myself next time to plan ahead. If I do not skip the meal but eat it far enough in advance so it does not interfere with my fitness program, which is four levels up the ladder on the pyramid, my chances will greatly increase for attaining my fitness goal. By satisfying lower level needs, for example eating, I will be able to attain higher level needs such as working out for self-esteem.

---

* see references

Self-fulfillment -------------------- Self-Actualization

Purpose and work ----------- Esteem and Satisfaction

Family and social ------- B e l o n g i n g

Residence ----- Safety and Security

Food and Water -- Physiological Needs

Returning to our organized views of content, have you ever taken the time to list your very own personal preferences? It is an exercise well worth doing and it helps much more if you put it in writing. This way you can review it from time to time to help stay "on course."

For example, if you place FAMILY at the top of your list, what have you done in the past, what are you doing in the present, and what might you do in the future?

Let's say you work for a big company and one day they offer you a good promotion with an increase in pay but it means relocating a considerable distance away from where you currently live. By taking a look at this concept BEFORE an offer comes, you can be better prepared well in advance. Ask yourself these questions and write down your answers in your personal success journal. If you do not have a journal yet, get one, because I promise you the single practice of journalizing can be one of the best investments of time you will ever learn.

For example, if the company offers you a raise, how much of a raise would it take to make your answer "Yes," knowing that you will have to sell your home and convince your entire immediate family on the concept, as well as the move. Think about it another way, what if the company is downsizing or relocating and they tell you that you can keep your present job but only if you are willing to relocate with NO raise. If you do not follow the company move you would be downsized.

Again, rehearsing these scenes in your mind prepares you to respond with much less emotion attached to the decision when and if the question arises. Most major corporations are impressed with executives and employees who decide quickly.

Suppose you are going to be downsized or have recently been released. How do you decide the next type of employment you really want? What if you have an O.K. job but are thinking about finding something new, different or better? Besides the actual job itself what will be the criteria you really want?

For example, some corporations place a very high value on employee health, as they know it reduces absenteeism and improves job performance. One of our local insurance companies has a fully staffed health and fitness club that opens well before the offices do and it stays open hours after the offices close. They have fitness trainers and even massage therapists (by appointment) at NO COST to qualified employees. Employees who are concerned with health LOVE this benefit. It would be almost impossible for a competitive employer to steal these employees unless they had similar facilities.

Regarding CAREER, do you just have a job for a regular paycheck? (J.O.B. stands for Just Over Broke). Or do you have a planned career path? Does your present position lead to regular promotions that will keep you happy? Do you know the company policy regarding promoting from within?

Do you regularly attend seminars and read books on self-improvement? Do you listen to self-help audiotapes in the car on the way to work? Do you regularly increase your job-related skills? Are you considerably better now than you were a year ago, or five years ago?

Do you know anybody in your company that is ahead of you on a similar path and who has been there five or ten years longer than you have? If you analyze where they are now, will you be happy and satisfied being where they are now, five or ten years down the line?

A lot of employees confuse ten years of new experience with one year's experience repeated ten times. Companies can only pay you more if and when you ADD MORE VALUE to the company and their customers each year. To paraphrase a popular quotation, "If you always do what you always did, you are already being paid all you are worth." So when you work on your career objectives consider these factors:

❖ What do you really want from your career? (Write it in your journal.)

❖ Where do you want your career to take you in one, five, ten and twenty years? What new skills have you acquired since you started with your present company?

❖ What new skills do the people who are higher up the ladder possess that you do not yet possess? Are you willing to do what they have done and continue to do? Be honest with yourself.

The vast majority of people with successful careers read a lot of non-fiction books, listen regularly to self-help audiotapes and attend continuing education classes for the rest of their lives. These are "works in progress" not 'finished up' or 'has-beens'. They have clearly defined career goals and objectives. Do you? Start today. (Additional recommended reading, Robert Kiyosaki's <u>Rich Dad, Poor Dad</u>*).

So far I have only touched on three of the many LIFE VALUES that will be covered in the following chapters. Start right now to make your own list of what you really want in life, including the five areas listed in the table of contents.

One method is to get a loose-leaf binder with tabs for each set of ideas. This way you can journal in each section as ideas come to you and be easily able to refer to any specific topic as you build you own blueprint for a fantastic life and joy in all categories. After all it is your life and you deserve THE BEST!

It is a good idea to have or work on achieving just one major goal at a time but you can have one goal in each of the five categories simultaneously. Just allocate some time to each one. For example, when I am at work I can ask myself "Is what I am doing bringing me closer to my written work goals or farther away?" When I am at home I can ask, "Is this the highest and best use of my family-time?" When I am driving my car, am I listening to the baseball game (tension relieving) or a helpful audiotape (goal achieving)?

There is a popular quotation, "Wherever you are, be there!" Do not take office work to the beach or on a family vacation. Plan well enough so your family gets

---

* see references

your undivided attention. So many people try to solve family or home problems while they are at work and then they bring some work related tasks home at night. On rare occasions there might be a legitimate emergency but if it is happens on a daily basis you need to plan better. Many companies have strict regulations regarding personal phone calls on the job. They know how calls negatively impact production of any kind.

Be honest with yourself. Do you work when you work and play when you are supposed to play? If not, what can you do to improve the situation starting today? There is a tremendous personal satisfaction in doing what should be done when it needs to be done, whether you feel like it or not.

It is important to mention again what Earl Nightingale, and later Brian Tracy, the famous author, both stated, "Successful people do the things that failures do not like to do." It took me a long time to realize that there is a lot of "stuff" that successful people do that they also do not like having to do (like cold calls, written sales expense account journals, follow-up letters, etc.) But they still do them because they know that they lead to more success later, just like the farmer knows that you have to plant in the spring if you want to harvest in the fall. It is part of the concept of cause and effect or sowing and reaping.

Successful people know the importance of doing WHAT needs to be done WHEN it needs to be done in order to reap the desired rewards, whether they feel like it or not, at the time. They know what the differences are between activities that are GOAL ACHIEVING, like the Olympic athlete who practices for four years, versus the 'wannabe' that sits on the couch watching the athletes on TV in a state of tension-relieving.

Whenever you plan a long journey by automobile, especially to a new destination, most people know the importance of a good map. It often helps to use a highlighter pen to mark the route. It also helps to have checkpoints along the way. If the trip involves an overnight stay it is always a good idea to make reservations before you start the trip.

Most people will do this for a vacation or business trip but few "plot the course" for their life. I find this fascinating. Remember that determining your desired outcome is the driving force for the rest of the seven important areas of your life.

CHAPTER THREE

Determining Your Desired Outcome

In order to get from A to B, (A being where you are *now*, and B being where you want to be at the end of a certain period of time,) you have to know several things. Let's do some "*homeplay.*" I used to call it homework, but I learned that "*play*" is more fun.

An acquaintance of mine, Lowell Jay Arthur, author of <u>Attracting Romance</u>*, used to teach a class in relationships where he provided a fill-in-the-blanks outline for participants, and to keep it light, instead of calling it a *workbook*, he called it a *playbook*. Following his lead, I have renamed practice exercises as *home-play* instead of *homework*.

Change can be fun when approached correctly. Many of my friends in Neuro-Linguistic Programming tell their students and clients that NLP really means, "**Now Let's Play.**"

Whenever you visit a large shopping mall there is usually a directory placed near the entrance. Somewhere on that directory there is a gold star or a red dot corresponding to the location of the directory. What does it say next to that mark? That's right, "YOU ARE HERE." This becomes "A", the place the journey begins.

One of the most important keys to gaining or regaining some semblance of control over our lives is to begin to make clearer pictures. Unfortunately, most people spend more time planning a one or two week vacation

than planning their life. To begin a more exciting and

rewarding life, there are methods we can use which have been tried and perfected by countless others.

How do most people plan a vacation or a cruise? For some, it begins with conversations about, "Where should we go?" or "What could we do?" then, perhaps a visit to a travel agent.

The first thing the agent will ask is (you guessed it!) "Where would you like to go?" The second is, "What would you like to do?" Then, if an airplane flight is part of the trip, the next question is, "Which airport would be most convenient for your departure?" followed by, "What is your desired destination?"

Many major cities have several airports servicing them. New York City has Kennedy, La Guardia and Newark. Los Angeles has John Wayne Airport in Orange County, and the primary airport, known as LAX or Los Angeles International as well as Ontario, Long Beach and Burbank Airports. So the questions again become "Where is 'A'?" (departure point), and "Where is 'B'?" (Where are you going?)

How does this work on a grander scale, our life-plan, our life-journey? First, we must clarify, "Where is 'A'?" Where are *you* right now?

Can you do a personal inventory or check list? Bob Harrington, the Chaplain of Bourbon Street, suggested many years ago to start each day by asking these questions to yourself:

The Morning Questions

Who am I?

Where am I Going?

What am I doing?

And later, I added, WHY?

Begin your revision by first taking stock. Do an inventory of your present situation. Put it in writing. Later, it will be a great source of joy, to look back and see the progress you have made and will be making.

When you planned your vacation, you used pictures and travel brochures to build excitement and anticipation. Doesn't your LIFE deserve, at least, the same level of effort?

If you do not have a camera, buy one of the great new disposables, with flash attachment, at a neighborhood drugstore. Take some pictures of anything important in your present life. Some examples could be: where you work, your family, pets, close friends, your house exterior and interior rooms where you spend the most time, your auto, sports equipment, anything that brings you pleasure and anything you want to change.

If you go bowling, add pictures of the place. If you fly, show the airport. If you fish, show the rods and reels and your favorite lake or boat.

Get a scrapbook or album and paste in the pictures. Write whatever comments come to mind. (Later, you will be adding newer photos from the journey, as you reach various significant checkpoints, just like the vacation photos.)

Write a list of comments and personal observations of your present situation. Just go for quantity, without judging if something is good or bad. After all, if it is in your life, it counts.

Then leave it alone for a few days. Your unconscious will process the data. Once this bigger picture forms, you will have a much better idea of where "A" is and where YOU are. This is a most important step, because you have to start with YOUR version of reality, not something told to you by others in your life. Once you are satisfied that you have a clear picture or pictures of "A" then it becomes much easier to plot your future course of action.

Many of the parts of the picture are very positive. It helps to write a checklist of the present conditions that you like and want to retain. Others are not serving you well and need to be replaced with more positive outcomes. One method is to take a clean sheet of paper, draw a vertical line down the center of the page and then put the "positives" in the left column and the ones you would like to change in the right column.

You can also create another visual aid by taking the previous list of morning questions and use the same style vertical line on another sheet of paper. On the left side of column 'A' list:

> Who am I?
>
> Where am I going?
>
> What am I doing?
>
> Why?

Then, directly opposite, construct your 'B' list.

A	B
Who am I?	Who could I be?
Where am I going?	Where could I be going?
What am I doing?	What could I be doing?
Why?	Why?

Once you have a clearly defined WHY, the HOW becomes easier. Each day review your 'B' list. Then, take an example from the movie business and construct a "storyboard". Get a large corkboard at a home improvement center. Start to collect pictures from magazines and with your camera, of where you want to be and what you want to be doing in one year and five years from now.

By reviewing your 'present' and your 'future' pictures, the route of your journey starts to take shape. Another good visual is to get a small map of the United States. Draw a line from Los Angeles to New York and another line from Los Angeles to Miami. Using a protractor (or just using your wristwatch) you will see that at Los Angeles, the angle formed by the two lines is approximately 30 degrees, like the angle formed between 1 o'clock and 2 o'clock. Yet the destinations are 1,300 miles apart.

A small change in your course, at the beginning, projected out over time and distance can make a very large difference in where you arrive. Keep this in mind as you construct your storyboard.

Take some of your desired outcomes and prioritize them, using a numbering system from 1 to 10, with the 10's representing the goals that will bring you the most joy. It is possible to have a lot of dreams and wishes in a variety of categories, but it is also more effective to have only one top goal in each category.

For example, you may have some or all of the following categories:

1. Family and Relationships
2. Financial Fitness and Security
3. Your career or ideal job
4. Spiritual Goals
5. Where you want to live
6. What kind of house
7. What kind of automobile
8. Physical Fitness
9. Etc.

Another method that works well, as mentioned earlier, is to assemble a loose-leaf notebook binder with page dividers and tabs, and a separate section for each category. This way you can list as many items as you want in each category and then put the most important item in each category at the head of each list. It then becomes easier to concentrate your laser focus on just ONE item at a time in each category until it becomes realized.

Anyone who has planned a long trip that requires navigating to new destinations, whether by private aircraft, a boat or an automobile, knows the importance of checkpoints along the way. This leads to MEASURABLE progress in reasonable time increments. We learn that there can be more joy in the journey than in the destination.

The most effective methods to realize your dreams always include CLARITY. Brian Tracy, the famous author, refers to this in several of his books and audiotape series[*]. By constructing your storyboards and your journals you become much more clear on exactly what you desire. A good "map" makes the journey a lot easier.

Recording your progress along the way also acts as a motivator. It is fun to reflect on the achievement of short-term goals and it instills confidence in our ability to do bigger and better things as we grow. Acknowledging an increasing competence achieving goals leads to greater confidence in setting our sights even higher.

Also remember that you are the producer, writer, director and star actor or actress in the movie of your life. You can decide where your own "yellow brick road" goes or where your own means of transportation takes you. With proper planning you can have a fantastic voyage.

Jim Rohn, the author and motivation speaker (see reference list), helps us to remember meaningful concepts with his vivid visualizations. He asks, "How long should your child spend in third grade? APPROXIMATELY?" The audience laughs. He continues, "Would most of you guess ABOUT ONE YEAR?" They laugh again. He adds, "Why do you think they make those desks SO SMALL?!"

He finds it humorous and at the same time somewhat sad that we expect "measurable progress in reasonable time" from all of our students but we are far too lax

---

[*] see references

when it comes to measuring our own progress, once we are out of school.

This is why keeping a journal or a written record of your goals, and reviewing them on a regular basis is so powerful. Small successes lead to bigger successes. The leaders in any field do not just do five or ten percent better than the averages, they do five or ten TIMES better, or more. They do not work ten times harder but maybe ten times smarter.

The recurring theme of this book is to optimize and maximize the joy you get to experience by realizing the little differences in effort and planning that yield the huge differences in results. Your rewards will always be in direct proportion to the goods and services you provide to others, your personal ability to ADD VALUE to the quality of life for others.

In Chapter 5 you will find an outline, a tool that can be used to help you with your desired outcomes. For now just put this chapter on a "simmer burner" and let your mind process it. One of the key principles of brainstorming is to SUSPEND critical judgement during the creative phase. Just let your mind soar and go for quantity of ideas first. Later you can see which ones make the most sense. When you get to the outline come back and apply it to these ideas also.

It also helps to remind ourselves that one of the reasons so many people lead what Thoreau described as "lives of quiet desperation," where we settle for far less than we could obtain, stems from fear of failure. After all, if "I do not set a goal, I can't fail."

Unfortunately, when we get older we realize that the biggest failure is simply not trying to improve the quality of our life. A lot of this arises from the advice of well-intentioned amateur parents who do not want to see us set ourselves up for possible disappointment. So they teach us to aim low and not try anything that might lead to setting a goal one cannot easily reach.

We, as adults, have to re-examine the childhood training to see if it is holding us back from realizing more of our potential. Many modern psychologists tell us that if you can imagine yourself doing better, you probably can as long as you are willing to do whatever it takes.

One of my favorite quotes is "COMPETENCE leads to CONFIDENCE." I started snow skiing at the age of thirty-two. My friends thought I was crazy and told me I could easily get injured. But, I had three small children and I wanted to convert our snowy winters into a source of joy for them. One of my dearest friends was president of the local ski club. I asked him for advice.

He said he would coach me if I agreed to join the ski club and take beginners' lessons. (At the time I did not realize that I would probably be the oldest 'kid' in the class.) I agreed. He took me shopping, showed me what I would need, measured me for all the equipment and gave me my first lesson in private.

Again, I learned competence leads to confidence. Once I learned, I was able to teach all three children and today the memories of the many family ski trips are among our fondest experiences.

On one of our several trips to Squaw Valley, I took the kids to see Lake Tahoe and the place where the "Bonanza" series of TV shows was filmed (older readers will remember The Ponderosa Ranch.) My oldest daughter had a love of horses. As soon as she was old enough she moved to Washoe Valley near Reno and became the director of The Sierra Nevada Handicapped Riding Association, a labor of love where she taught countless numbers of handicapped children to ride horses.

Because of this wonderful work many years ago, she received a gift of intuition and the ability to communicate directly with animals. She has received national recognition. Check her out at www. terrijay.com. It started because I summed up the courage to take ski lessons. You never know exactly where courage will take you and those you love.

CHAPTER FOUR

Knowing

One of the five primary areas of content is KNOWING. Not since the times of the ancient Roman Forum and the Greek philosophers have the fields of KNOWING and KNOWLEDGE become so important to society. With the rapid advances in the development of computers, most experts agree that we are now in the information age.

It is fascinating for the students of change phenomena to review the tremendous progress that has taken place just within the span of this past century, which many attribute to the turning of the millennium, the year 2000, as if this round number contains magic of its own. It reminds me of watching the odometer in an automobile as it rounds off a large number with a lot of zeros.

Why has this particular span of the past 100 years been so significant? Students of history will tell you that societies go along for about 400 years with little change and then the next 100 years includes more changes than the preceding 400 years put together. Let's review the past century.

In the early 1900's, our society was primarily an agricultural one. Some statistics indicate that 93% of the total population lived on farms. People grew their own crops, built their own homes, made most of their clothing and were relatively self-sufficient, with perhaps the once-a-week trip into town, with many towns being not much more than an intersection with a few local merchants or shops.

With the coming of the Industrial Age many people went to work in the factories as physical extensions of the machinery. Automobiles started to appear and then airplanes. Internal combustion engines made it possible for one farmer and a tractor to do the work of several farmers. Electric motors and conveyer belts made the factory assembly line possible. Blue-collar workers outnumbered farmers for the first time ever in history.

This created the need to manually process all of the data. Later this led to an increase in white-collar workers, who outnumbered blue-collar workers after World War II ended and we returned to a peacetime economy. Service industries began to take up the slack. Retail businesses expanded and in the late 60's, as time became more precious, we saw franchised fast food shops emerge.

While a lot of this was taking place we had the benefits of telephones and quality radio, then television and computers. Now, we have fax machines and modems that give access of the information super-highway to anybody who is willing to invest a few hundred dollars. More recently we have cordless and cellular telephones and satellite communications, using man-made "moons" orbiting the earth. We have laptop computers, battery powered and many with wireless access to the Internet. We have palm-sized computers with more built-in power than regular computers of just a few short years ago.

Paralleling this progress, we saw vinyl records replace the old phonographs with home stereo music systems using first 78's, then 45's, and then 33's. This seven billion dollar a year industry is now extinct, replaced by technology that is affordable to the masses. After the invention and demise of eight-track, we had audio cassettes, miniature tape recorders, automobile stereo systems, books-on-tape and most recently, CD's and D.A.T. (digital audio technology.)

To me the most amazing part of all of this is the constantly accelerating speed of change, which has become exponential. The famous book by James Redfield titled, <u>The Celestine Prophecy</u>* suggested that the product of the year 2000 and beyond, would be information, rather than "things," or tangible goods. Automation, computerization and robotics will make all of the things we need, using fewer and fewer human beings in the process. What will all these displaced people do to earn a living?

For one thing, they will all have the choice of continuously updating their personal knowledge and skills, or they will be left behind to do the unskilled or semi-skilled work that remains, where it is still necessary to utilize humans in the process. With time, fewer numbers of workers will be required.

It is still a pleasure to go to a fine restaurant and have the staff serve you with a personal touch, although in the kitchen the food may be prepared in a microwave oven. (Incidentally, for many single parents, people living alone, or couples where both work full-time, the microwave and prepared frozen food make it possible to eat at home with a minimum of time spent preparing the food to be served.)

A quick scan of your local yellow pages advertising will show you that there are still hundreds of service businesses around that do require the human touch. The challenge is for the former factory worker and former middle management workers who are being

---

* see references

squeezed out of the work force by technology and corporate downsizing or rightsizing to retrain for different jobs. (No matter what you call it, someone who formerly had a decent paying job is now out of work, regardless of the PR department's name for it.)

When I graduated college, more years ago than seems possible, if you had a college education in a profession, you felt like you were set for life. Perhaps you would attend a yearly convention and hear what is new and you would be set for another year. Not any more.

Latest figures suggest that the typical person graduating college today may have six or seven different careers during a 40-year work life from age 25 to 65. These are not just different jobs, but different careers.

I have watched the technology and information explosion in my own former primary profession of eye-care. When I graduated college, most hospitals had an E.E.N.T. clinic (Eye, Ear, Nose, and Throat) and you can still see some signs on the walls of older hospitals.

I cite this only as an example of just one area of health care. E.E.N.T. practice meant one doctor taking care of any problem in these four areas.

Then eye doctors separated out of E.E.N.T. and became known as *oculists*, leaving E.N.T. to someone else. As the information grew, *oculists* and newer graduates took additional years of training in medicine and surgery and became board-eligible and board-certified as *ophthalmologists*, who could and would take care of anything involving the eyes, including exams for glasses, treating disease and all forms of eye surgery.

Today, just in the field of medicine for the "Eye" we have:

1. Corneal specialists
2. Cataract specialists
3. Vitreous specialists
4. Retinal specialists
5. Laser surgeons (some overlap into cornea, retina and cataract)
6. Refractive surgeons who clarify refractive (vision) errors to reduce the need for glasses and/or contact lenses.

This is <u>just</u> in eye-care. There is so much new technology that it is virtually impossible for any one person to know everything that is going on, even in one "niche" market. It is small wonder that sometimes we suffer from "circuit-overload" in our brains.

Referring back to the <u>Celestine Prophecy</u>, it becomes all too obvious that we will indeed have to pay someone for what they know since we cannot possibly learn all about everything in this lifetime. Our only defense is to become an expert in one or more areas so we will also have information and skills for which others will be willing to pay us, so we have something to trade.

I remember laughing during commencement exercises at college, when one of my colleagues said, "I am so sick and tired of school, that when I graduate, I am *never* going to read another book." Poor fellow.

What are our choices? Let's apply part of the formula for Neuro-Linguistic Programming to this challenge. What is my (your) desired outcome? What do you want? Remember the quote from a children's book, "If you do not care where you are going, it does not matter which road you take."

Because KNOWING is not at the head of the list for everybody, many will just choose a line of public service requiring the least amount of continuous education. That is their right, yet in my research I find it difficult to find many fields of employment where this applies.

Starting with the letter "A" I spotted "Auto Mechanic." I went to visit the local new car dealership service department. They have so much electronic diagnostic equipment for everything from transistorized ignition testing to laser frame and tire alignment that I thought, well, auto mechanics have to have continuing education just like computer scientists do.

Then, I looked under "B" for Barber Shops. After all, a haircut is still a haircut, or is it? Not really, in most places it is now a hair styling. If you choose to do anything about the color of your hair, the operator nearly needs a Ph.D. to be sure they do not do anything that could result in a lawsuit.

One of my acquaintances owns several salons. All of his employees and associates, in order to keep their jobs, must attend one full Sunday per month of training classes, lasting from early morning until late in the evening, on new trends and styles.

He is financially very successful and attributes a large part of that success to continuous training of staff members. He says that although some may complain about giving up one day extra per month, the conversations of staff with clients and customers proves that they feel more confident and professional.

About the only place where a lot of continuing education is not required is in the occupations where someone does the same thing over and over, like working on an assembly line. Not surprisingly, these are the jobs that are most easily replaced by a robot or a computer. So, it appears that continuing education and learning new things is essential and very beneficial.

How do you know when you know something? How can you be sure that you know something? In acquiring knowledge (that which is known) there is a four-step paradigm through which most learning experiences travel.

First, we start out as *unconscious incompetent*. That means we do not know what we do not know. We are ignorant of the fact(s).

Second, we become *conscious incompetent*. We discover that something exists about which we have no knowledge or inadequate knowledge. Then, one of several things will happen. Perhaps we will decide that we do not need to learn it (the old sour grapes fable.) Or, we can put it off ("I'll study that later.") Or, we can acknowledge that this is something we want to learn and will begin the process of learning it.

As we go through the learning process we come to the third level, *conscious competent*, we know how, but we have to think about it as we do it. The fourth level is *unconscious competent*, we just know that we know, as in the following example:

A sixteen year old child (with no driving experience) tells their parent, "I want to drive the car." So, to begin the process, the parent puts them behind the wheel in the driver's seat and hands them the keys. Their first reply (remember, no prior experience) is, "What do I do, first?" When they asked if they could drive the car, many think it is so easy. After all, they have watched someone else drive countless times. They are at the **first level**, *unconscious incompetent*.

They do not know that they really do not know how. When they ask, "What do I do?" they become aware that perhaps they need to be told or taught. This is **level 2**, *conscious incompetent*.

After some lessons, they eventually are able to drive, by recalling all of the many steps involved, as needed. They are a **level 3**, *conscious competent*. Then, one day, it all automates, they just get in and "Drive the car," having reached **level 4**, *unconscious competent*, because they no longer have to consciously think about each step.

I use this illustration of the KNOWING paradigm to help understand that this process is normal. Once we fully grasp the concept, it becomes easier to acquire any additional knowledge and any additional skills necessary to be able to function the way we elect to function on a daily basis.

The next logical level is to understand why we want "to know." What will that additional information *do* for us? You begin to see that all of the areas of content have some tendency to overlap.

Many of the more recent books on "motivation" mention the importance of clearly defined goals. The following example, attributed to a Yale University study, shows how important having written goals can be for you.

In 1953 the graduating class members were asked, "Who has written goals on their person (in the wallet for the man and in the purse for the woman)?" Only three percent responded in the affirmative.

Twenty years later, at the class of '53 reunion in 1973 the people who had written goals in 1953 were asked to state two things: "How much do you earn per year and what is your net worth now?" (What you own minus what you owe.)

The rest of the class was asked to answer the same two questions. Here is the startling conclusion:

The three percent who had written goals in 1953, earned more in 1973 than the other ninety-seven percent combined and the same ratio applied to their net worth, that is, the three percent had a combined net worth greater than the other 97%.

For me, this statistic certainly illustrates the importance of clearly defined goals, in writing. I learned this lesson back in 1962 when I read Laws of Success[*] by Napoleon Hill. This book was the predecessor to his Think and Grow Rich,[*] read by millions of people.

Hill originally called this step #1, "Having a Burning Desire." This was later relabeled "Definiteness of Purpose." In NLP, we ask, "What is the desired outcome, stated in a positive terms? (Towards goals, what you want vs. away from goals, the things you want to avoid.)

To get greater clarity on the importance of KNOWING, it helps to ask yourself these questions, "Why do I want to know this? What will it do for me? Once I know this, how will my life be different? What will change?"

---

[*] see references

You see, there is a major set of differences between a "wish" and a "burning desire," as Hill called it. Some students wish they could know a school lesson so they can pass a test, get a grade and return to something else that is more fun. Others want the knowledge because they believe it will enrich their life, while still others see particular subject knowledge as "means" to different "ends."

As the information age expands, anyone who wants to play the game that is being played today (and it almost seems to change daily) is aware of the increasing importance of knowing. If you do not particularly enjoy memorizing facts and figures it helps to know where to find the data you may be required to locate.

Einstein stated, "I do not choose to memorize anything I can look up. Why fill my head with useless data?" Obviously, the key is to know how to look it up, and where.

Harvey Mackay, author of two famous books, <u>Beware of the Naked Man, Who Offers You His Shirt,</u>[*] and <u>How to Swim with the Sharks,</u>[*] says that one of the keys to his success is the use of Rolodex™ file systems. He has more than 6,000 names of valuable contacts, people he met over a working lifetime. He tells the story about negotiating with the publishers of his first book regarding how many copies should be run on the first printing. This number greatly influences the cash advance and the chances of becoming a rapid bestseller.

The story states that when he started to pull his Rolodex files out from under the table and started

---

[*] see references

naming company presidents, CEO's and the number of employees at each of these companies whose leaders he knew personally, the number of books for the first printing was negotiated up by a factor of *ten times* the usual, virtually assuring the success as a best seller.

By knowing so many people and by knowing how to convey evidence of this to the publishers, he assured his own success as an author. So, one of the methods you can use to increase what you know is to develop your own filing systems.

Today, may people carry palm pilots or laptop computers with built-in systems, which can later transfer data directly to their larger desktop computers at home, or at work. With the increasing complexity of the Information Age, a method for storing information and retrieving information is a must.

In review, KNOWING means not only acquiring a lot of facts, figures and formulas, but also understanding the "six true friends" of Kipling and every news reporter:

WHO? WHAT? WHEN? WHERE? WHY? HOW?

and the methods for applying the data towards the accomplishment of your predetermined worthy goals or ideals. This requires a systematic method for storage and retrieval, designed to help you accomplish what you want.

Since one of the primary purposes of NLP is learning how to "model excellence," we can all learn from any experts we select. If we follow Napoleon Hill and select our "burning desire," or if we follow the Yale University study and become part of the three percent with written goals, clearly defined, written or typed on paper and carried on our person at all times, we greatly increase our odds for success.

If we follow the Rolodex system of Harvey Mackay or use it as a pattern for our own method of data storage and retrieval, then acquiring and accessing necessary data becomes a fun game.

It is also essential to decide the difference between "means" values and "ends" values. For example, money to buy a new car is a "means" value. The car which seems to be an "end" is also a "means" value. For if we use the car to take our family on a vacation, it becomes a "means" of transportation. Once we are on the vacation, we can all have a good time and feel better, perhaps acquiring some peace of mind. That state is the real desired "end" value.

Keeping the ultimate desired "end" in mind often provides us with the strength, courage and determination to acquire whatever we need to KNOW to make it possible.

I recommend the book <u>Core Transformation</u>[*] by Conniray and Tamara Andreas as an excellent self-help book which teaches the reader how to tell the differences between core states (end values) and the steps along the way which are often confused with the real goals.

EXERCISE:

　　1.　How important to me is KNOWING?

　　　　Rate from 1 to 10 (10 is most, 1 is least.)

---

[*] see references

2. Write down 3 goals you want to reach, and by WHEN.

A.   DATE:

B.   DATE:

C.   DATE:

3. How much time will I allocate each day to increase my knowledge by reading (non-fiction) or listening to audio tapes? _____ (Hours, minutes) per day.

4. A. Which of the suggested books in this chapter will I buy or get from the library first, after I finish this book?

Title _____

B. By what date do I intend to do this?

Date _____

5. List as many benefits as I can, of how increasing my knowledge will help me achieve my goals.

_____

_____

_____

_____

_____

_____

_____

_____

_____

_____

_____

_____

_____

Remember:

Everything Begins With An Idea

It is important to realize that knowledge alone is POTENTIAL energy, like water above the dam. Only when the water is directed to and allowed to flow through a turbine generator does it produce useful electricity. Your knowledge has to be put into some sort of plan, followed by action. Calvin Coolidge stated that the world is full of educated derelicts. (Knowledge alone does not guarantee success, but it is also very difficult, if not impossible, to have great success without knowledge.)

One of my favorite jokes was told to me by the manager of one of our largest public libraries. A serious looking college student approached her at the reception desk and asked, "Do you have a self-help section?" She replied, "We have a very large one." He asked, "Would you mind showing me where it is?" She replied, "Wouldn't that be self-defeating?"

Taking the initiative to obtain knowledge is the first step. Knowledge, plus a plan of action, followed by action and persistence, leads to success.

CHAPTER FIVE

Being

One of the primary divisions of CONTENT is the area of BEING. As children, we all heard the often repeated question, "What do you want to BE when you grow up?" We also often make a joke with some of our friends who are in mid-life career crisis by asking them the same question, meaning of course, "How do you want to spend the rest of your life, from this point forward?"

Dr. Wayne Dyer, the famous psychologist and author, advises to ask yourself, "Am I a spiritual being having a physical experience, or a physical being having a spiritual experience?" We believe that we are all spiritual beings but some of us have not yet personally made the discovery. Zoologists classify us as Homo-sapiens, modern man, human beings, the only living species of the genus Homo. The emphasis of course is on human BEINGS.

One of Shakespeare's most famous quotes is "To BE or not to BE, that is the question." If we are physically present, then we are in a state of being. The verb "to be", is one of the most difficult to conjugate, because it has so many forms. Just ask any foreign-born student of English. I am, you are, he or she is, they were, he was, she will be, they have been, etc.

Here are a few notes from the dictionary. BE: to exist; to happen or occur; to remain or continue; to come to (May God *be* with you); to have a place or position, etc. The list is very long. Spend some time with your favorite dictionary and construct your own list of definitions and examples. It will enable you to have a broader perspective of how important what you choose to be or become will influence and impact the rest of your life.

Whenever you see any of the examples in a written sentence or hear them in conversation, we are referring to BEING or becoming something: past, present, and/or future, singular or plural. When you were younger, what did you want to BE? Can you recall?

How did it turn out? Have you fulfilled some or all of your earlier dreams? Are you happy being who you are and what you are today? Do you plan on being different, tomorrow, next week, or next year?

As mentioned earlier, I used to be very overweight. My father was in the wholesale food business, selling dairy products to the neighborhood grocery stores. I remember complaining to my mother about the fact that we had to eat eggs every day. She said, "Be glad he is not a shoemaker, we could be eating leather." I blamed my childhood for my weight challenge for years. Then, one day I just decided to be thinner.

I read every book I could on the subject of weight management and behavior modification and decided once and for all to BE thinner. I started to pay attention to what BEING fat was doing for me (the hidden positive intention.) How did I think anything was going to be different if I kept on with my old habits? Insanity, as defined by many programs, is doing the same thing over and over and expecting different results. I knew I had to do the things that thinner people did so I could BE thinner. I started to honestly count calories and fat grams as a percentage of the total, eventually lowering the fat to twenty percent or less. I also started a modest exercise program and was amazed at how good it felt.

I talked with people who looked and acted physically fit. I decided I wanted to BE like them. From that point on, I have never gone back to being the former way.

I use this only as an illustration. In Neuro-Linguistic Programming, one of the best tools for change-work is called the "Positive Outcome Frame". I first learned this when I studied with Dr. Richard Bandler, the original co-developer of N.L.P. Other pioneers in N.L.P. contributed to the final form. (see Reference List.)

So often we go through life blaming others or circumstances for anything that is not ideal in our lives. It is only by assuming full responsibility for how we CHOOSE to react that we regain a sense of control.

Make a copy of the outline first, to use as a "Master" because you will want to use this as a template for any time you want to make important changes and improvements in ANY area of your life. Whenever I do consulting or coaching with clients, whether one-on-one or with a group, I find that the template produces rapid change and lasting change for improving the quality of your life.

Now, let's start to fill in the blanks as they apply to BEING, assuming that you may want to BECOME different from the way you are now.

THE "POSITIVE OUTCOME" FRAME

1. WHAT do you really WANT? (Stated in POSITIVE terms, what you DO want, not what you do not want.)

_____

_____

_____

2. HOW will you KNOW WHEN you have it? (What sort of evidence will let you know?)

_____

_____

_____

3. A. WHERE will you be doing this?

_____

_____

3. B. WHEN will you be doing this?

_____

_____

3. C. WITH WHOM will you be doing this?

_____

_____

4. A. What are the BENEFITS of your PRESENT behavior? (That is, what are the benefits of NOT changing?)

_____

_____

4. B. What are the COSTS of the NEW behavior?

_____

_____

4. C. What are the BENEFITS of the DESIRED behavior? (Indicates level of motivation. The longer the list, the better.) Use the back of this page if needed.

_____

_____

5. What STOPS you from accomplishing what you want?

_____

_____

_____

_____

6. What RESOURCES do you PRESENTLY have, towards the new desired outcome(s)?

_____

_____

_____

_____

_____

7. What ADDITIONAL RESOURCES do you need? (Comparison: Going on a vacation, packing lists.)

List A. What I already have. (Same as Number 6, above)

List B. What else do I need to get?

_____

_____

_____

_____

_____

What is your FIRST STEP towards making it happen?
(TAKING ACTION!) Whenever you decide to do
something new, always take SOME action step the very
same day, even if it is just to call an 800 number for
information.

_____

_____

_____

_____

_____

By referring to your new journal or your loose-leaf
book of GOALS it becomes much easier by using this
outline to once again create your very own map, your
personal plan for progress and personal growth.

Here is some additional information to use when
completing the outline.

Re: Question 1. There is a difference between
TOWARDS goals and AWAY FROM goals. Most away
from goals are fear-based, like I do not want to lose my
job or my breath, etc. These weaken you. Towards
goals are more like moving toward the carrot or the
reward for accomplishment. You have probably heard
the quotation "where ATTENTION goes, ENERGY
flows."

It seems that poor people worry about the things that
can and do go wrong and they seem to get more of
what they fear. Successful people focus on what they
want and they get more of the good things in life. It
requires deciding moment by moment, day by day.

Question 2. This refers to EVIDENCE procedures. For example, if one of my desires is a new car I will know that I have it when I see it parked in my driveway and the new sticker is still in the window.

Question 3. Where, When, and With Whom... Answering these will help you visualize your desires more clearly and raise your energy levels.

Question 4 A. This is a question seldom asked by people who have difficulty with change. Every behavior has a positive intent or intention for something in our lives but it might have a negative outcome. Until we discover or uncover the benefit of NOT changing, that benefit will sabotage our efforts. The classic example is the overweight person who feels bad about being overweight but who feels good temporarily when he or she eats something sweet or fattening.

Question 4 B & C. Once we understand that the benefits outweigh the costs, it is easier to "pay" what is required.

Question 5. You have to recognize the stumbling blocks and turn them into stepping-stones. Learning from our mistakes makes us stronger and smarter.

Question 6. Think of going on a vacation trip. You may already have a lot of what you need to take along. When setting goals, most people will desire something that is attainable, something that is well within their means of reaching. If you can imagine it as possible for you, it is usually achievable. Start with your present skills, abilities, and past successes list. Build on these.

Question 7. As far as additional resources, remember the role models. When you read about others who have reached the goals they wanted, what resources did they have that you could also acquire?

Earlier I mentioned the importance of SELF-IMAGE. When you change, when you become the person you want to be, as you get closer to the desired outcome, your self-image WILL GROW.

Recently, one of the most outstanding marketers of our time, Dan Kennedy, acquired the rights to the life works of the late Dr. Maxwell Maltz and thanks to Mr. Kennedy and Nightingale Conant Corporation you can once again learn about self-image from Dr. Maltz via audio cassettes. This is a great series to own and listen to repeatedly as you change who you are now to the person you really want to BE.

As you acquire more self-confidence, marvelous things begin to occur on a regular basis. As Dr. Maltz stated, "everything you do must be consistent with your own self image." Carefully decide the characteristics of the ideal person that you want to be, use the outline and the tapes and BECOME that person.

Again, the more competent you become, the more confident you become. Competence leads to confidence. When you become more confident you will discover that you can BE anything you choose. If you are willing to acquire the necessary skills that the person you want to be should possess, virtually anything is possible.

CHAPTER SIX

Doing

One of the five areas of primary concern to Americans is DOING. In our frenetic society, we all seem to be too busy, because we have so much to do.

I am always amused when I visit an appliance shop or a gadget shop and see all of the so-called labor saving devices. They range from automatic laundry machines to electric apple peelers and illuminated pepper mills, battery driven for portability and with a down-light so you can see where the ground pepper falls on your salad.

The first question that comes to my mind is if we have all of these time-saving devices, how is it that we have LESS free time?" One answer is that nature abhors a vacuum; humans do not like to be bored or unoccupied for any length of time, so we find things to do.

We seem to be happiest when we fill every minute with some activity, yet so often the things we DO produce little lasting satisfaction. My studies illustrate several principles or reasons why this is so. One reason is because we perceive time as finite. After all, there's only 24 hours in a day, right? So if we don't DO IT NOW, perhaps it might not ever get done. Never mind, if the time might be better spent doing something else.

When it comes to DOING, Americans are busy people. We love to DO things. We take our work and our careers seriously. The same is true for our hobbies and our activities after work.

Often you will hear someone say, "I have SO MUCH to do, and so LITTLE time!" Well, the truth is we each have the same twenty-four hours in a day. The difference is what we DO with our time.

Many years ago, I believe it was in the 1920's, a gentleman named Ivy Lee was hired by the president of a major steel manufacturing company, as an efficiency expert. It seems that all the executive staff had way too much to do and that the pressure of unfinished tasks at work frustrated them.

Mr. Lee observed the situation and told the president, "Here is what I will do. I will show you how to greatly increase everyone's effectiveness and efficiency. Try my method for thirty days, and then pay me what you believe the plan is worth."

At the end of the trial period the president of the company paid him $25,000 for one idea. In today's dollars that would be worth somewhere around one million dollars. What was the idea?

The "To-Do" list. Mr. Lee taught them to "spend a few minutes before leaving in the evening, get a clean sheet of paper and LIST, in writing, the five to ten most important things you want to DO, tomorrow. Sort them in the order of importance. Then, tomorrow, start your day with Item #1 (here is the key) and DO NOT go to the item 2 until item 1 is FINISHED! If you get interrupted as often happens to executives, as soon as the interruption is over, go back and Finish #1 before you start on #2.

There is a tremendous power to this technique that is not initially apparent. First, you are making the list the day before, in a calm, cool, collected mind-set, without the telephones ringing or people barging into your office. Often this is created after most other employees have gone home for the day. Your ability to prioritize is not burdened by trying to do multiple tasks while deciding on what to do first."

Next, there is a real sense of accomplishment as you check off each item on your list as being finished. I used to draw lines through the project descriptions. Then, I switched to using a highlighter so I could still see what the item was after it was finished. If I ever felt frustrated, from time to time, I could look back at previous lists and reward myself for all the things I finished.

Make a To-Do list binder and at the end of each day you review the list and bring forward any items that are not finished yet; you re-prioritize and redo the new list so you are ready to start the new day with the items you selected the evening before.

It is possible to have "To-Do" lists for work and "To-Do" lists at home too. On the one for home you can include the daily tasks like meal preparations, shopping, etc, AND you include the recreational activities as well. This can be coordinated with your daily planner for scheduling but the difference is that the To-Do list helps you decide WHAT to do while the planner tells you WHEN.

Always allow a little slack because unexpected events do occur. The list does help you get back on track a lot quicker. People who are organized get much more out of every day. It is also o.k. to give yourself permission for some BLANK blocks of time so you maintain some level of flexibility and the ability to be spontaneous. I call this my "free-time" and I reserve it for any kind of fun that comes up.

Julia Cameron, the author of <u>The Artist's Way</u>[*] advises the artist's date, a block of time where you get to "recharge you own batteries!" Maybe there is a show at a local art gallery and no one other than you wants to see it. She says go alone and enjoy it, without guilt and without worrying about what some other person wants to do or see. You deserve it. Maybe there is a good movie only you want to see or some hobby pursuit. This is the ideal time to enjoy it. You will come away energized.

Exercise:

Make a list of ALL the things you think you have to do. Separate into work or job related, home activities, and pure fun activities of things you WANT to do. Perhaps three separate lists will be required to do this. That's o.k. Then you will discover how to create free time. I use a process I call "selective abandonment." From time to time I remove items I no longer enjoy doing.

A friend of mine used to spend several hours a week mowing his lawn and not because he enjoyed it. His wife sold the lawnmower to a neighbor's teenage son who wanted to have his own part-time business. The condition was that he would mow their lawn on a regular basis for a satisfactory price. The husband could then abandon the project and acquire several extra free hours per week to do whatever he wanted. At first the husband complained. But once he saw that the young man enjoyed doing a great job, he relaxed and had much more fun pursuing his own hobbies, using the time that he formerly spent mowing the lawn.

---

[*] see references

Or maybe you could reduce the amount of time spent shopping. Some time ago I joined a network marketing company that has a virtual mall with thirty five million products and a lot of well-known national vendors. As a "rep" I actually make commissions on my own purchases. It is a lot of fun and saves time, too. I can make purchases in a matter of minutes at home and have the products delivered. Compare this to getting in a car, going to a store, finding a parking space, and taking the time to make a purchase. I can use the time saved to DO other things that have a higher priority and are more rewarding.

Following the exercise, review each of your lists. Try to prioritize each activity, on a scale of one through ten or simply A,B,C, etc., with the A's and 1's having the highest payoff. After you have your ABC list, divide the B's into A and C and then throw out or delegate all of the C's.

Most readers are familiar with the 80/20 rule. As it applies here, 80% of your pleasure and satisfaction comes from 20% of your activities (the A's). See which of the 80% of your C's only contribute 20% of your satisfaction and get rid of all that you can, so you have more time for the A's.

For example, my staff used to take a lot of time to get necessary office supplies from the store. Now, we order on the Internet in a matter of minutes and the next day the products arrive by UPS or FedEx. When you factor in the cost of employees' time, the Internet saves a lot. This is especially true for products you use routinely so you know your preferred brand, and the prices paid in the past.

Because I am in healthcare and still seeing patients, I have a daily schedule with time blocks of units of fifteen minutes each. A patient might require one, two, three or four units, depending on the nature of their visit.

This type of schedule makes you acutely aware of the value of time and what you are DOING at any given time. I have a separate schedule for my activities outside of work but I also cross-reference important after-hours activities on the appointment book at the front desk.

There are many excellent planning systems to keep you aware of what you are doing. I recently attended a lecture featuring a time management expert and he advised a month-at-a-glance overview so you can pencil in important activities ahead of time to avoid schedule conflicts. He then dovetails this with a weekly page and if more information is required, a daily page.

His entire system fits easily into a mini briefcase that he carries with him at all times. He also schedules most of his recreational activities so he has plenty of time to do the things he needs to do and also to do the things he wants to do.

This way he is able to do a lot more with much less pressure. He also blocks frequent DO NOTHING periods to recharge his "mental batteries." These are used for fun activities that he feels he has earned.

Did you ever sit down with pen and paper or at the computer to list all the things you LIKE to do? Here is a real good, fun exercise, based on research studies of state lotteries' big winners.

A very large percentage of big lottery winners after a few years claim that winning the lottery was the worst thing that ever happened to them. For many, the relatives and friends who wanted or demanded a "piece of the pie" was more than they could handle. Many had to leave their circle of friends who were envious and move so far away that nobody followed them and then start over.

Just for a fun exercise, ask yourself: If you won millions of dollars, what would you DO then? Make a list in writing. Would you move? To where? Would you still want to go to work on a regular basis? Doing what? How would you spend your twenty-four hours a day? What would you do then that you feel you cannot do now?

Once the wish-list is finished, go back and ask yourself (be honest), "Even if I never win the lottery, which of the things that I really want to DO, could I make plans and change part of my life NOW, that would enable me to DO the things I really want to DO?!

Often you will be amazed to discover how changing your thought process can bring more joy more quickly than you thought. For example, one of my young clients loves to go fishing and boating. He discovered that by going back to school and becoming a licensed ship's captain, he now spends spring, summer and fall sailing a charter ship on the Great Lakes. He feels like a millionaire playboy. In the winter he goes back to his former occupation and remodels home interiors. Now he buys fixer-uppers, repairs them and sells them for a nice profit.

If he won the lottery he might drop part of the winter job, but he would still want to sail and fish eight or nine months a year. So, now he does it without being a lottery winner. He is one of the happiest people I know because he is DOING what he loves.

What could you do that you love and still earn a living? Think about it. It is much more fun, once we get clear, DOING the things we love to do.

Can you go back to school or acquire new skills to bring more fun to you on a daily basis? This is worth thinking about and then DOING something to make the necessary changes. It is far better to look ahead now with excitement than to look back at age sixty-five with disappointment. As always, it is a CHOICE. What can you visualize yourself doing differently in one year, five years and ten years? Will you DO it?

CHAPTER SEVEN

Getting and Having

Most people love to shop, to buy nice things, to get them and have them to enjoy. It has been my observation that people would rather buy the things they WANT than to buy the things they need.

I recently had a patient arrive in my optical shop on a Saturday evening just before closing time. She had a nice pair of bifocal eyeglasses and the frames had just broken. She informed me that the glasses were not from our place, but could we possibly repair them for her. She said she wears them all the time, from the time she gets up until she goes to bed, seven days a week because she "needs them to see."

I asked her, "Don't you have another pair to use, while we repair or replace your frames?" She replied, "No, because I only use one pair." Since she was sharply dressed, I then asked, "How many pairs of SHOES do you own?" She said, "Don't go there!" I smiled and asked, "Why not?" She answered, "Because you sound like my husband. I have about 40 pairs of shoes, almost one to go with each of my outfits or colors of my wardrobe, to match the clothing and the occasion.

The shoes are all over the closets and my husband always complains about them, because there is no room for his "stuff." I love to buy shoes, but I HAVE to buy glasses to see. It is more fun for me to buy shoes and imagine how nice I will look and how much fun I will have when I wear them." She was smiling as she must have recalled one or more dressy affairs where others complimented her on her appearance and her wardrobe. We did an emergency repair and then I convinced her to stop back and start to build her wardrobe of designer eyewear, as another fashion accessory to complement her wardrobe. I asked, "What do you think other people see FIRST, your eyewear or your shoes?"

At first she was puzzled because in all her years of wearing glasses, not one person asked her that question in selling her a pair of glasses. The more she thought about it, the better it seemed. I reminded her also that the new eyewear wardrobe would be fun, functional and take up a lot less closet space than all of the shoes. We both had a good laugh.

The main point is that people do enjoy buying nice things and using them. Marketers and advertisers have known for years that if you can first create the desire and then convince the consumer that your product or products will satisfy that desire in a superior manner, you sell more with greater pleasure, and you increase the opportunity to make sales.

For example, when I was growing up Station Wagons with wooden side panels were introduced as the ideal family vehicle with room for all your kids and their things. When Lee Iacoca was president at Ford Motors he realized that the Baby Boomers did not want to drive their parent's big fender sedan. He introduced one of the most successful cars of all times, the Ford Mustang Convertible. I vividly remember because I can still clearly picture my yellow Mustang convertible with the all-leather interior and the big engine. In those days owners said it was HOT! So did my sixteen-year-old son who begged me to let him use it.

Later generations said, "Hey man, what a cool car." All I know is that it was a lot of fun to drive at a reasonable price. At that time it was a bit of a status symbol to have the first one in the neighborhood.

So, what are some of the most efficient and effective ways to get and have more of the things we say we want? As previously mentioned, most of us have virtually unlimited wants. So how do we determine how to get what is referred to as, "more bang for the buck," a best return on our investment of time and money?

I vividly recall taking a course in economics back at Ohio State University during my undergraduate work. In those days, "economics" was defined as "the science that deals with peoples' endeavors to satisfy UNLIMITED WANTS with LIMITED MEANS, capable of alternate usage."

For example, if I see two objects I want to buy and they are each priced at $100 and I only have one hundred dollars cash it becomes immediately clear that if I do not want to go into debt I have to decide which one I want most, and buy it, but not the other one, at least not at this time.

This is classified as an economic decision, choosing for the greater result. It is a priceless lesson to learn, no pun intended. So often however we are sold on the idea of get it now, just charge it, no payments for a whole year, etc. This is how consumers and countries get into such huge credit problems. Although there are legitimate times when it does pay to use credit to make a purchase, most of the time, especially for consumable goods, it represents a major mistake. I will show you why and how a little later on in this chapter. There are a lot of things the credit card companies do not want you to know.

For example, why would anyone who is still working, buy a certificate of deposit that pays a return of 2 or 3 or even 4% and then charge purchases on a credit card? This means you are lending money to the bank at that low rate. They then turn around and give you a credit card carrying rates from 8-9-10 up to 29% if you miss ONE payment. It is extremely essential that you read all the fine print on all your credit card statements. I will show you some real eye opening examples soon.

When is it okay to buy things you want on credit?

One is a Primary Residence. You are going to live SOMEWHERE and pay rent, probably for the rest of your life. So it makes economic sense to take your present rent payment, if renting, and investigate how much of a home (if you like yard work and exterior maintenance) or a condo unit (pay a service fee if you don't like yard work) you can afford and do all the numbers.

The people who sell condos will do a lot of this for you. Remember that early in the ownership, the majority of your monthly mortgage payments will be tax deductible from your ordinary income. Do not be misled by this. Even though the entire INTEREST amount is deductible, your personal saving, for fair comparisons, is only your TAX BRACKET times that amount, not the whole thing as suggested.

For example, if you have a proposed $1,000 a month mortgage payment and the first year (just for comparison) it is ALL interest, if you are in a 30% tax bracket you do not save $1,000. You only save $300 per month on your income tax. Also, the amount saved comes down every year as more of your payment is applied to principle.

However, in all fairness, this means instead of paying $1,000 a month rent, you could probably afford $1000 per month on a home, and use the $300 savings toward real estate taxes and/or condo fee. You also have to calculate the cost of homeowner's insurance required by the mortgage holder. When you deduct all of these expenses it is often less expensive to just rent, but with a few very good reasons NOT TO.

1. Rents do not go down, they usually go up over time due to inflation.

2. Property values can and often do go up with inflation, as a hedge, too. If you are buying a home or condo, once your mortgage payments are set up with a fixed rate 15, 20, or 30-year plan, your monthly payments remain constant, unlike rents.

   Assume I buy a $200,000 condo in a brand new development with only 10% down, as new units are built the price is usually higher by 5 to 10% per year. If well maintained, the value of the original units also goes up. However it is important to realize that the TOTAL increase in value is based on the TOTAL price, NOT just your down payment.

   If I put down $20,000 and the price then goes up just 5% in one year, that means the value goes up $10,000 (5% x 200,000). Since I only put down $20,000, my $20,000 is now worth $30,000, a 50% increase or 50% return on my investment!

   If the new ones go up 10% (not unusual in a well-planned large development) my down payment of

$20,000 is now worth $40,000, a 100% return in just ONE YEAR! So, it pays to do your homework.

For example, when my father passed away twenty-five years ago, we sold the family home, invested the net proceeds, and moved my mother into a new apartment nearby. It is now twenty-five years later. Her rent, which started out at almost $250 a month, is now almost $800 a month, more than her monthly social security check.

I mention this primarily so when you go to make your decision to buy or rent, you consider ALL the variables. While no one has a real crystal ball, the statistics are available at any library or on the Internet regarding the history of inflation over the past several decades. Overall, it goes up. My first four-door Cadillac sedan was $3,200. The similar model today is over $40,000. Just be aware of the trends.

I believe that no one is going to care more about your money than you will, or should. Yes, learning about money, finance, and real estate investing involves a lot of time and effort, but I guarantee you, it will be worth it. After all, it is your money.

Of course, I believe in having an excellent group of experts on your team. If you are not an attorney, you need to know a good one. The same is true about an accountant and someone who knows real estate law.

If you like to invest in the stock market, you need to have a good broker who understands your personal life plans. That leads to the next subject.

What are your personal life plans? As mentioned in earlier chapters, if you want to get and have more of the available items in your life, it begins with written plans.

Some philosophers are teaching that less is best. Simplify, simplify, simplify... if that is congruent with your personal philosophy it confirms for some believers that THINGS do not guarantee happiness.

For others, possessions can be a great sense of joy. It is an individual matter to decide.

It has been my observation that planning to buy the things you want or need, doing some homework (or home-play) and comparing what is available greatly increases the satisfaction of acquiring nice things. It also reduces the risk of "buyer's remorse," buying something on Monday and by Thursday or Friday seeing something similar that you would have preferred or for a whole lot less money if you had known about it on Monday.

It is fun to be spontaneous and just buy some items for amusement, when you see them. Some experts say the best way to do this is to set aside or budget a small percentage of your income for these types of purchases so you do not go overboard or spend money that is needed elsewhere in your budget.

For example, I love to travel to distant places. By having a place in my budget for travel, I have been able to visit countries from Australia through Hawaii to my west and Spain and Great Britain to my east. As soon as I return from a great trip, I start planning for the next one, by budget, so I do not feel guilty.

I mentioned earlier the extreme importance of fully understanding the pros and cons of credit cards. It seems that the number of personal bankruptcies continues to climb and one of the leading causes is spending more than you make.

Here is a simple exercise that can possibly save you from financial disaster. If you truly want to get and have more things, one of the ways that secretly robs you of having more is the money you just might be wasting servicing credit card debts. Do not take my word for it. Do the following exercise and convince yourself. You will thank me later, because the money you used to waste can then be used to enrich your life.

This exercise is simple but you need to do it on paper, and make sure you use a calculator for accuracy. First, get out the last statements from ALL of your credit cards and if there is more than one, spread them out on your kitchen table. You may need a magnifying glass to see the small print as it appears in different locations on each statement.

The next step is to look at each statement until you find the INTEREST that they charge you per month. Also note that some credit cards have MORE THAN ONE rate of interest. For example, one rate for purchases and one for cash advances or to pay off other credit cards may all range from 8% and up. Search them all out and mark in bold ink on the top of each statement the various rates of interest.

Next, sort out the statements, if you have more than one card, by looking at the highest interest rate card FIRST. We examine the highest rate card first because as we start to get rid of the balances, one by one, we want to save the most money possible in the shortest amount of time.

At this point, we want to locate on this first statement for review, the amount marked MINIMUM

MONTHLY PAYMENT and write it on your worksheet (the blank sheet of paper). Next, locate on the statement the TOTAL FINANCE CHARGES for that statement. Now, subtract the FINANCE CHARGES from the MINIMUM PAYMENT. What is left is the REMAINDER that will apply toward your principle. At that statement's date, your balance will only be reduced by the amount of the remainder. The rest of your payment is lost to interest. Now, pour yourself your favorite beverage, take a sip, then breathe deep, and let's continue.

Using your calculator, divide the REMAINDER into the TOTAL BALANCE. For example, if the minimum payment is $100 and the monthly interest is $80, the REMAINDER is $20. The total balance is $2,000. 2,000 divided by 20 equals 100. This means that if you do not buy another thing on this card until it is paid off, it will take you approximately 100 monthly payments just to pay off this debt. If you divide 100 months by 12 months per year, you are looking at 8 years and 4 months to get out of it and only if you cut it up right now! (It will be slightly less, as the card is paid down, a little more goes toward principle and a little less toward interest, but I just want you to get the overall picture of how you can easily dig yourself into a hole.)

The next step is to take the minimum payment times 100 months and it comes out, in this example:

100 months X $100 =

$10,000 to pay off $2,000 worth of debt!

Even if the shift from interest to principle cuts the time in half, you will still pay $5,000 to pay off a $2,000 purchase. And, you could have used the extra $3,000 to get and have something else, instead of giving it away to the credit card company for finance charges. Why would you want to pay even $5,000 for a $2,000 purchase?!

If you want the EXACT numbers take the time to go to the bank, set up an appointment and ask a bank official or loan officer to calculate exactly:

A. How long will it take to pay off the balance if you just made the minimum monthly payments per month?

B. What is the TOTAL DOLLAR amount of all the payments added together?

C. Then just subtract the amount you owe now, from that number. The rest is ALL FINANCE CHARGES, money you could spend on more important things!

You can then see why it is so easy to get credit cards. As long as you pay on time each month, banks hope you NEVER pay off the balance in full, or stop and realize just how much money you are giving away to them.

Although it may be disheartening to see just how one credit card can affect you financially, it is important that you do this with ALL your credit cards. Being honest with yourself is the first step to overcoming debt and living a life of financial freedom. As you write down the numbers in your journal, ask yourself what else could you enjoy if you also had all that interest money to spend on things you really want by paying cash.

The final step in this exercise, and this is a BIG one, MAKE A PLAN to pay off all of the cards as fast as possible. Yes, you CAN do it, in less time than you think at first glance.

When I lecture on this topic I ask my audiences this question: If you are not self-employed, if your employer said, "We have a financial challenge. I can either lay off 10% of all employees (without identifying who they would be) or if everyone agrees to a voluntary 10% pay cut for one year, everyone gets to keep their job." Which one would you choose?

Rather than run the risk on being one of the 10% to get fired, the VAST MAJORITY selects the 10% pay cut and keeping the job. This proves the next part.

Most people (not all) could find a way to tighten the belt, cut back on a few luxuries, eat at home more often and consume less fast-food or restaurants and manage to get by. Some might add a part-time second job to get by on 10% less on their primary job.

This proves that for those of you who really understand, you can take that 10% and month by month apply it to pay off the first credit card principle as fast as possible. The trick is to still pay the minimum payments on the other credit cards while purchasing necessities with cash. It is very important to become committed to not buying anything else on credit; wait until you have the cash.

Then some magic takes place. As soon as the first card is paid off, you take the 10% and what you used to pay on the first card (now gone!), use this amount to add to the minimum payment of the second card. The second card should be the next highest according to interest rate. It disappears much quicker than the first one did.

If you have a third, when the second is gone, you take the 10% plus what you had paid monthly on the first AND second and apply ALL of this to the minimum payment you were making on the third. MORE MAGIC!

Soon, they are all gone and you develop the habit that if you do keep one card for convenience, you pay it in full every month. You then start to save for all future purchases and pay cash. You will never go back to the old way because real peace of mind is priceless.

Once you are on a cash basis you can begin to more effectively budget to acquire all the things you really want. When I got out of college, high fidelity stereo sound equipment was just becoming popular. I really wanted a system. In college I had a radio with very poor speakers. Now that I graduated I wanted the best. I started to work at an audio company on Sunday afternoons from one to five p.m. I became an expert on the equipment and helped the owner by offering to install systems we sold to the new customers. I agreed to be paid in sound equipment at wholesale cost. Today I still have some of that original equipment with free standing dual speaker cabinets and fifteen-inch woofers that you could use to break any lease. It still sounds fantastic and I enjoy the fond memory of working at a new audio company to earn it, not going into debt. I enjoy things more if they are paid for in advance.

The equipment serves to remind me that if you really want to get and have nice things, a little ingenuity goes a long way. I was also able to buy one of the first commercial model three tube projection television sets. It had a six-foot screen that first appeared in the sport's bars. It is a lot of fun to watch sports in the comfort of your own living room on the big screen.

A wish list or want list can be used to motivate yourself to do whatever it takes to purchase the things you desire, especially if you do so WITHOUT going into debt. As the title of the book suggests, it gives you a sense of control.

CHAPTER EIGHT

Relating and Relationships

One of the reasons why it is so important for us to establish relationships today is that there are very few areas of our life that when we get involved, we are not relating. We have relationships at all different levels.

Most of us realize that we want to get and have better relationships. By the time you finish reading this chapter, you will have many more tools for building better relationships.

Why do we have problems or challenges as I prefer to call them, in an area of our lives that most psychologists believe should be a natural, easy process? As the first example of relationships, I want to use the American dream of romantic love.

We learn from the fairytales, where the knight in shining armor comes to rescue the fair maiden and take her off to Never-never Land, or when you kiss a frog and he turns into a prince and you live happily ever after. Nowhere in the fairy tales do you read anything about doing dirty dishes, making beds, cleaning the house, or changing the baby's diapers.

So we start out with a myth. We wonder why the fairy tale doesn't come true. That is just one type of relationship, but it is the one that usually comes to mind first when we think about relationships because it is a sought-after ideal.

In romantic love, there is the storybook individual we want as our partner in intimacy "till death do us part, forsaking all others." At least that is how it is supposed to start out in the beginning. There is a funny story about a woman who went to court to see about getting a divorce after being married for forty years. The judge asked her, "Whatever happened to "till death do us part?" She replied, "Your honor, when that was written people only lived to be thirty or forty years old, so it was no big deal. But today, enough is enough."

Let's take a look at some evidence. Depending on which statistics you read, somewhere between fifty and sixty percent of all first-time marriages end in divorce. Of the rest who do not divorce and remain together, a large percentage admit to being very unhappy in the marriage and only a small percentage experience the marriage as a source of joy, ecstasy, and satisfaction, which most of us say we would like to have. Why is this so?

After a period of time, some people lower their standards and expectations settling in many cases for a mediocre relationship. Why? For one thing, that is all we have seen all around us. This is how we have been taught to relate by our role models. Since this method does not work a high percentage of the time, maybe we could or should investigate some other ideas or methods.

This section will help you to develop new models or methods of relating based on more recent discoveries of how and why our present methods fail and what are our options. What do I mean by "modeling"?

One of the major turning points in my life occurred several years ago. I was out of school, had a degree in optometry, and bought a practice which I later discovered had a terminal illness; it was dying. I was fortunate enough to have a friend that took me to hear a gentleman named Earl Nightingale who gave a speech at that point in time called, "The Strangest Secret." (I mentioned this earlier in Chapter 1 but my primary emphasis there was on financial success. Now, I want to illustrate how the same concepts apply to relationships.) It was later released on record (that was before cassettes) and sold over a million copies. It was the largest single-selling phonograph record that didn't have music on it. It's now available in cassette form through Nightingale-Conant.

That night for me was a major breakthrough in my life. The message contained two basic factors. One, we become what we think about. "As a man thinketh, so he becomes." Second, is the danger of conformity. Earl spoke primarily about financial success. He stated that fewer than 5% of the total population reaches age 65 with an income anywhere near what they made while they were working. The rest were essentially flat broke here in America, the richest country in the world. His point was that if we role model after just about anybody the odds were 19 to 1 against picking a successful role model.

The same thing is true today with relationships. If we model after just about anybody, and 60% of marriages end in failure, then we just might be copying the wrong person. I got to know Earl personally many years later when I sponsored his radio show, "Our Changing World," in the Cleveland, Ohio area for almost five years. It was then that I asked him why he called it, "The Strangest Secret." Let me repeat the answer from Chapter 1:

> Well, it is strange to me is that I'll explain it to 100 people and only five people will take the lesson and do something with it. The reason I

call it a 'secret' is because it might as well be a secret because nobody knows about it and even if I tell them they still don't know about it unless and until such time as they incorporate some changes in their lifestyle.

We think of ideas like the water above the dam that just sits there until it goes through the causeway and forms electricity through the generators. Like the dam, we hold onto these ideas, like potential energy, but until we put them into motion nothing happens. They might as well be a secret unless we employ them on a daily basis.

How many of us would let a seven-year-old run our life? I don't think too many of us would do that knowingly. Seems foolish, doesn't it? Here's a fact: Most of us were taught what we know about relationships between the ages of zero and six or seven. We were raised by amateur parents unaware that they were conducting a training class because babies do not come with an operations manual. Even a computer comes with a book that tells you how to run it and a toll-free phone number for additional help if needed.

Generally over 50% of the people in my speaking audiences come from homes where their parents were divorced sometime before they were out of the house living on their own. They didn't have substantial role models to relate to, therefore, what they learned was not good. Of the remaining 40+% whose marriage didn't end in divorce, I find their marriages are a compromise. These are the kinds of things I hear:

"He/she is good to the kids."

"I can't afford a divorce."

"He/she is a good provider."

"Our religion forbids divorce."

Or it is a matter of low self-image. Either the husband or wife will say that their spouse is better than they deserve and they are lucky to have someone to care for them and share with them. Sadly, they settle for a little less than what they think they should have.

Lastly, there are those that worry, "Who knows, the next one could be worse." Nobody wants to trade a headache for an upset stomach!

So when it comes time to build our own relationships, even though we haven't had the greatest of role models to identify with, we beat ourselves up wondering what has gone wrong. Yet so often, we have an inner feeling that there must be some way to have better relationships and friendships. Some of us believe that we should know how to do this automatically, but it is a fact that relating to another person is a learned skill.

It is something that can be taught and something that can be learned. As such, it's possible to learn how to have wonderful and empowering relationships that do fall in the win/win category where the combined value of two is greater than the sum of individual strengths separately.

What are some of the other kinds of categories or relationships that we could or should experience? As I mentioned before, we are looking for joyfulness. We want ecstatic, satisfying, rewarding relationships. Because we all have to work for a living, there is the employer/employee relationship. How can we make this a harmonious situation where we don't dread going to work every day? (Which can kill you, by the way, but I'll cover that later.)

We also have to relate with co-workers. How many times are there conflicts on the job? How many people will quit a job because they can't get along with their fellow employees? Or sellers and customers? How many times have you heard or felt that you could have handled the last transaction differently? We have problems with customers and sometimes customers have problems with sales people who are having a "bad" day and want to dump on somebody.

These are our relationships and our success in our career very often is dependent on our ability to build good relationships. In the past sales trainers would teach "features and benefits." You buy the features and you buy the benefits. You don't buy the drill, you buy the hole that the drill makes.

Today all professional sales trainers are talking about building lifelong relationships where you become part of their team. You go in as a problem solver where you're helping the other individual solve their problems and then they buy your products because you have built a relationship with them.

We also have to look at family relationships, children and parents and in education, students and teachers. Why all this trouble with relationships? In the early 1900's more than 90% of the total population lived on a farm and everybody knew their job. The family unit was essential to survival. A farmer and his wife would have children and they would stay on the farm and take care of them when they got older. Many generations lived in the same household. We didn't have the problems that we have today in relationships. People just got along out of necessity.

It's amazing but in a country where there is a lot of internal fighting going on, when they are invaded by another country all of a sudden they unify. It's "them" against "us" instead of "us" against "us" especially if it's essential to survival. We have a hierarchy of needs. Survival ranks number one and everything else follows.

With the advance of the Industrial Revolution, people went to work in factories. Cities got larger and we tended to specialize. People became less independent and more inter-dependent. For instance, very few people build their own homes anymore. They hire someone to do that. We don't make butter any more, we go to the store and buy it. We're dependent on the products and services of other people.

As technology advanced, fewer and fewer people lived on farms. Today the number is less than 5% of the total population that produces the crops for everyone else. With the Information Age and with television, things have reached the point where turning back is almost impossible.

For many, living in the suburbs is an attempt to go back to nature and the soil even if the only things they plant may be the front lawn and the flowerbed. In spite of all the labor-saving devices that we enjoy, for many the quality of life is just not that good.

Computers have depersonalized our society. How many people have a PIN number? We don't even get to go into the bank anymore and converse with the teller, we just pull up to a machine and put our card in and push the buttons so we've lost again a chance for a personal relationship.

My mother is up in years and is considered legally blind. She went to the bank in a local shopping center and asked a new teller to please fill out a check for her because, as she explained, she was legally blind. She continued explaining to the teller that if the teller would point out the signature line, she could sign her name on it so that it could be cashed. The teller followed her directions and out of rote asked her for identification, particularly a driver's license!

There has been a tremendous shift in our society most recently about what is really important. Our values are changing. We're attacking the cores of many of the issues that we have taken for granted in the past. Now we're really taking a look at those things because we want to have more meaning in our life.

We have electronic computerized dating services because we don't have time to play the dating game. Yet people are hungry for people to talk to, to be with, to build relationships with. But since most of our present methods do not work, where and how can we find better models? Two interesting areas, believe it or not, are quantum physics and human psychology.

In the field of psychology, one of the most powerful is NLP or neuro-linguistic programming. When I attended Nightingale's program many years ago, that started me off on a quest to find out that why it is that so few people succeed in the richest country in the world. I've been studying all kinds of psychology, motivation, philosophy. I've been able to work as a consultant in very large health care practices sharing that information with other people to help them take their struggling practices and turn them into very successful operations.

Very briefly, our brains process information with very specific patterns. These patterns can either provide you with the keys to successful living or they can direct your behavior without allowing any conscious choice. So often we turn the controls over to automatic pilot and we don't necessarily achieve those things that we say we want to get.

Richard Bandler, the co-developer of N.L.P. and author of several books, often asks, "Who's driving the bus?" In other words, we're going down the highway sixty miles per hour sitting in a back seat and we look and there is no one at the wheel! Very often we are on automatic pilot because the brain will roam and it doesn't really care what you seek out. Since relationships are a form of human behavior the study readily falls in the domain of psychology which is defined as the science of mental processes and behaviors of an individual or a group. In the past 30 years three new distinct schools of psychology have had their followers and each group has made an impact and made advances on the study of what makes us tick.

The first is Gestalt psychology which was founded by Fritz Perls. Basically, the term "gestalt" comes from the German and it means a "complete entity" a total circle filled. The theory that Perls had was that most of the neurosis and psychoses that people develop come from missing pieces. If we try to decipher something and if we envision things in pictures and part of the picture is missing it is very hard to know what it represents and we wind up with frustration and tension.

Author Deepak Chopra states, "If we are at ease, that's the opposite of dis-ease." That's where the term comes from. If you have all the pieces of the puzzle you can look at it and understand what it represents. But if some are missing you don't have closure. What they try to do in Gestalt therapy is to go back into the past, find the missing pieces, and complete the puzzle so that you can get on with the rest of your life. It's a very effective technique.

The second one and more recent field is Transactional Analysis (often abbreviated as TA) based on the work of Eric Berne and Thomas Harris, and exemplified by the books, Games People Play[*] and I'm O.K. You're O.K.[*] TA has three parts called ego states referred to as Parent, Adult, or Child (P, A, C). Because it is transactional analysis they define the transaction as any communication between two people from one of their ego states. Each ego state serves a specific function and we can all identify with these.

The Child ego state is where all the feelings are. It's the five-year-old playing outside in the winter making snow angels, totally oblivious of the temperature and the weather. When adults do that they are said to be in their Child ego state. That's where all the fun comes from. All of us have seen a child walking along in the springtime and they see a puddle and they go stomping through it so they can watch the water splash off in all directions, just having fun.

The Parent ego state contains all the tape recordings that we received early in our lives by our well-intentioned parents. And those things are buried back

---

[*] see references

there and will kick instant replay at a moment's notice if the circumstances justify it. These are the injunctions: "'You should," "You must," Don't ever do that again." All of these injunctions are accepted as gospel because we receive them before the age of reason. We have no judgement at that point in time. So if mom and dad who are keeping us alive tells us, then it must be true.

And far too often well-intentioned parents tell a child something that the child buys into for the rest of their life and it blocks them, like "You're stupid" or "You're clumsy" or "You're dumb." Just in a sarcastic comment someone will make that statement and the child will go through the rest of his or her life saying, "What do you expect from me, because I'm stupid or dumb or clumsy." And they'll fulfill that role for the rest of their life without going back and taking an objective look at that behavior.

Many never realize that they learned that behavior when they were 6 or 7 and maybe since they have acquired a few new skills in the last 10, 20, 30, or 40 years. Yet they buy into it. That's why we called it an injunction. We follow them blindly.

Now some are beneficial like, "look both ways before you cross the street." Saved my life one time in downtown Cleveland. I was crossing a one-way street and I looked both ways and a guy was backing up 35 mph the wrong way. So they are not all bad. Sometimes they can be valuable like, "Don't touch the stove, it's hot." Those would be classified as "parent tapes" stored in the back of our mind, things we heard and learned from our parents. It's interesting to note that when we behave like our parents we are said to be in our Parent ego state; the pointing of the finger. Telling kids to don't do this and don't do that.

Now in analyzing the transactions, if communication takes place with matching ego states from Parent to Parent like a couple of women talking about what's going on with their children and respond back Parent to Parent then the transaction is said to be parallel, meaningful communication takes place. But if the transaction is crossed it is like someone talking down to you.

For instance if a husband asks his wife what time it is and she responds "7:30" and then five minutes later he asks again what time it is and she responds, "I just told you five minutes ago. Why don't you wear your watch!" This is Parent down to Child – cross, anger. No longer is meaningful communication taking place. So that's one of those things that when they are analyzing a transaction it's a good skill to have because you can tune in and hear what's taking place and find out whether these transactions are parallel or not.

Now the Adult ego state which is at the middle acts like a kind of computer. It's takes in information from the Parent ego state and feelings from the Child ego state and it estimates probabilities in the process of making decisions. Here's a perfect TA example:

An adult male is playing ball with one of the children having a great time, literally reliving a slice of his own childhood. Now the ball rolls out into the street, a car is approaching, the Parent ego kicks in and reminds him to look both ways before you cross the street. The Adult ego state kicks in, estimates the distance and the speed at which the car is approaching and computes that there is enough time to go out and get the ball. He retrieves the ball and comes back, the car goes by safely and the game is resumed, back into the Child ego state. So in a matter of seconds they go from Child to Parent to Adult to Child. So it's a real good way to analyze this type of scenario, to understand what's taking place. You can learn all about that in the book, I'm O.K. You're O.K.

In T.A., the "I'm O.K." refers to the metaphor that has to do with self-image and self-esteem. In the book it tells you how to differentiate what's going on with people. The book draws something called the O.K. Corral, where there are 4 different ways that people can interact.

I'm OK You're OK

I'm OK You're NOT

I'm Not OK You ARE.

I'm not OK and you are not OK either.

It explains how people get into these places and get stuck there. It interferes with how they get along for the rest of their lives. If they have inferior feelings they tend to have much worse relationships than if they feel equal to other people. The only good state is I'm OK You're OK.

In the early 1970's Richard Bandler, as I mentioned, teamed up with a professor of linguistics, John Grinder. They developed Neuro-Linguistic Programming psychology which in my opinion is a quantum leap ahead of everything else that has ever come down the pike because it works very quickly. People trained in NLP can do a one-hour phobia or trauma cure that lasts. They've taken people that have been in therapy for years and cured them in a couple of sessions, permanently. And they test for the cure.

I saw a demonstration of a gentleman that had a fear of heights and as a salesman couldn't go past the second story of a building because he was afraid of elevators. So if he was selling something and a client's office was up in a building, then he had to call another salesman to come in and make the call.

After being treated with a particular NLP method or technique, he was taken over to the Hyatt Regency next door, put in the glass elevator which is on the outside of the building and taken up to the Polaris Lounge. When he came back he discussed with the class what had taken place.

Someone in the class commented that "You've had a life-long fear of heights." He responded, "That was a long time ago." The man replied, "It was this morning." The other man replied, "Well for me, now that's a long time ago." This is the kind of things that can be done in the NLP therapeutic modality.

NLP psychology is a toolbox. It's a method for understanding how we process our data using our five senses as filters because we do filter our data. We record this information as subjective experience because there is no power in words except that which we give them. But in our experiences we can describe our observations and have pretty fair agreement as to what is taking place.

NLP is the study of the structure of subjective experience. It is used to develop methods for modeling excellence in any and all fields of endeavor.

The approach began actually many years before NLP by a man named Alfred Korzybski who wrote a book called *General Semantics*[*]. Our brain uses a process of abstracting. Dr. Deepak Chopra in his books states that less than one billionth of all the sensory stimuli that are around us get through our system and are recorded in our brain. That's done for protection so that we don't suffer sensory overload.

There are three basic categories that we use for filtering our data. One is called **deletion**. For example, someone asks if anyone has seen their car keys and someone else says, "Yes, they're right there in front of you on the table." That's a deletion just like a computer, when you push the key; first you see the letter or word and then you don't.

[*] see references

The second one is **distortion**. Have you ever heard a water faucet dripping late at night and you're trying to fall asleep and it gets louder and louder? It doesn't really get louder; if you checked it with a sound meter you'd find that the sound level was exactly the same. But our brain distorts that sound to motivate some kind of action so that it can get back to a peaceful mode. Usually we'll get out of bed and shut off the water.

The third method of processing data is **generalization**. Some very popular generalizations would be "starting the car." You get in and you start the car. If you had a sixteen-year old who had never driven a car and you wrote down the steps to start the car you'd have a page full. Generalization is a very convenient shorthand method for our brain to process information.

Now think about all the things that you do every day. Many of them are generalizations: brushing your teeth, doing laundry, watering plants, putting on your shoes, etc. Have you ever driven to work or the grocery store and wondered how you got there? Generalizations work very well as efficient methods for getting more things done, without thinking about the individual steps.

In NLP we also talk about mapping our experiences. However, remember the map is not the territory. When you are at a restaurant, you don't eat the menu. The menu is simply a word description. A map is a word or picture description as well. Think about the different kinds of maps you have relied on at one time or another. If you had a street map and directions then you could follow it to your destination.

However, if you look at the map and then look out the window at precisely the same location, they do not look anything alike. The map is an abstraction, a graphic representation of what is outside the window.

We, too, record information in our brains in maps. It's not the experience though. We can learn in NLP how to change our map, thereby changing our recollection of the experience. We can't change history but we can change the recollection of the history or the map. One of the reasons people have problems in communications is because different people have in their head different kinds of maps.

Think of both a highway map and an aeronautical map. They can both be of the same area yet look completely different with specialized language and symbols because they have different purposes. One is for cars and one is for airplanes. They can't be interchanged. People need to understand each other's maps by finding some common ground before they can have meaningful communication and before they can build relationships.

NLP also operates on an unconscious level, too. In this deepest structure are the things that take place in our minds that cannot be put into words. This is the representational system based on our five primary senses: hearing, sight, touch, taste and smell. In NLP these senses are referred to as:

Auditory

Visual

Kinesthetic

Gustatory

Olfactory

or abbreviated, AVKGO.

Although we all have five senses we have different priorities. Three people are told about a situation. One replies, "Sounds good to me." The second replies, "Yes, that feels right." The third says, "Looks good to me."

Obviously, the first is AUDITORY, sounds good. The second is KINESTHETIC, feels good. This is the person that when shopping for fresh fruit or vegetables, has to TOUCH several before selecting what they want to buy. The third is obviously VISUAL.

Again, NLP is the study of the structure of subjective experiences in all areas of life. On the third level, where we choose the words we say about the images, sounds, sensations, movements, smells, and tastes, we often get into trouble with our communication. We describe those but the description is not the substance. It's a process that human beings have been given. We want and need to be certain that we are on common ground when we are discussing something with somebody else and not to be a mind reader.

For instance, we shouldn't assume that if we taste something and find it sour that everyone else will agree. If it tastes sweet to them, communication begins to break down. We filter things through our five senses. We have words for describing these. Now a metaphor for this is a new island being formed over in Hawaii and it's almost 30,000 ft. high from the bottom of the ocean but it hasn't broken through the surface yet.

Korzybski initially described our deep inner feelings that influence our behavior. They are like the molten lava that is in the center of the earth. It is breaking through the floor of the ocean, completely invisible to the people on the surface, building this huge mountain under the water and then one day it breaks through the top. Experts feel that if it continues growing at its present rate then it will be bigger than the island of Hawaii. Ideas and experiences can be like that too.

Emotionally, we have a deep inner level, a transition level, and then we have the level that's above the surface for everyone to see and to make comparisons. That's how our brain processes data and we abstract, or use words, to describe this data. We get involved in semantics, or the meaning of the words, and unless we are on common ground we are not going to have good relationships. Here's a perfect example:

An executive walks down to the factory floor and asks a foreman, "How are you doing?"

The foreman responds, "You don't care."

"Yes I do. That's why I asked," replies the executive.

"Well I took a class in body language and you're standing there with your arms folded and that means to me that you're closed. You don't care. You're just asking to be nice."

"No," insists the executive. "I just came down from a heated office and you're down here wearing heavy clothing. I'm cold. I'm just trying to keep warm."

What happened was a total misinterpretation on the foreman's part because he misread the signs. Once you understand these techniques, you'll have many more tools, patterns or recipes, to make better choices.

Let me illustrate with a metaphor. Suppose that you asked me to come over to your house and to experiment making bread. Should be a simple task. On the way over I stop at the store and I buy a bunch of stuff that I think I remember reading on a bread label one time. When I get there we begin to try, at random, different combinations and by midnight we still don't have any bread and I leave with both of us disappointed. Sound like a first date?

What else could we have done to guarantee at least an edible loaf of bread? One thing we could have done is to get a cookbook or a recipe. Secondly, find out what are the ingredients we need for this specific recipe and buy those ingredients and get them together. The third thing would be to follow the recipe and combine the ingredients in the proper quantities, in the proper sequence. The next thing would be to have the proper size and type of pan to contain the bread that we are making. We would need to give the yeast time to rise. Sometimes it takes overnight. We might have to start on Friday to make bread on Saturday. Another critical factor would be to preheat the oven to the proper temperature and bake the bread for the proper amount of time.

Here's a ten-step process to make something as simple as bread. Do you think that a relationship is worth investing in the same type of process? The secret for better relationships is to study excellent relationships for the key ingredients and the combination.

Remember, NLP is the study of the structure of subjective experience and its application to modeling excellence. Just as a recipe greatly increases your success in baking bread, NLP can show you how to get consistently good results in getting, building and keeping better relationships.

Let's pretend that we are in a beginner's cooking class, but what we are going to cook up is better relationships. If whatever recipes or methods you have tried in the past did not produce the desired end results, get and read a good cookbook. Learn from the most successful people you know or can read about.

The NLP definition of insanity is "doing the same thing over and over again and expecting different results." In this culture if something doesn't work we do it either harder or more; like the government who starts a project by giving it a million dollars and if it doesn't work they give it two million dollars. If whatever you're doing doesn't work then do anything else because obviously that isn't working so don't keep banging away at it. Try something different!

There's one other thing that people in our society tend to do. That is that we are blame oriented. We want to blame somebody for all the things that have happened to us in our lives. Unless and until such time that you assume full responsibility for where you are today then that means that someone else is responsible for making you feel good. Someone else is going to have to be responsible for changing your life.

I don't necessarily mean that it's "your fault." What I mean is that you have to assume responsibility for the way you are because another definition for responsible is "response-able." If I take charge of my life, and I assume responsibility for where I am today that empowers me to make whatever changes are necessary so that I can get to a different place.

As long as we continue blaming other people because I'm mad at someone else, because they made this situation as bad as it is, I have to wait for them to do something in order for it to get better. Which would you rather be, empowered or at someone else's mercy like a puppet on a string, a victim so to speak?

If being a victim is something that we should avoid, then where do all the "professional victims" on daytime TV come from and why are they so prevalent? "Because they get paid!" would seem to be the obvious answer. However, there is a segment of the population who loves to go see disaster movies.

Going back to the *I'm O.K., You're O.K.* kind of thing then: if they can find someone worse off than they are then it makes them feel somewhat O.K. by comparison. Even in the bottom of the Great Depression there was a story called *The Grapes of Wrath*.* These people had nothing. So by comparison people felt that, "we don't have it that bad."

There are people who judge themselves not by how they feel but by how many people are underneath them or worse off than they are. That makes them feel relatively O.K. by comparison. I know people that do not watch the late night news because they don't want to go to bed with all those negative stories. There are no good news stories though, because they are boring. People won't pay money for those. Look at all the magazines along the supermarket cash register with their negative headlines. It's unfortunate but there are people that feel good when they read something bad because it makes them feel O.K. by comparison. They wouldn't have to, if they are O.K. about themselves in the first place.

Speaker Wayne Dyer, told an audience that I was in, that we are ALL winners because at the moment of conception there is one egg cell and millions of sperm and yours was the winner! So you start out as a winner because the other millions of sperm didn't make it!

In the works of Deepak Chopra, we understand and teach and learn that BLISS is the normal state for people. However, we let so much garbage into our lives. We actually let people control us with our permission! We say, "In order to be a doormat you have to lay down on the floor." The only way that it can happen is if you lay down and be a doormat.

We let these things happen because we don't have good role models. When we hear something before the age of reason we accept it as the absolute truth, unless and until such time later on, we find out that there are other more efficient, more effective methods for dealing with those issues.

Maybe everything that we learned as a child wasn't true! It shakes your foundation. When I was a child in second grade they told us that you can't take away 5 from 2. When I was in 5th grade, they said, "Sure you can, we have negative numbers." I was so furious with the teacher that my mother had to come to the school because I cussed at my teacher. For 3 years they had been lying to me!

In the typical cross section of the American public many people are not mentally fit. Murray Banks, a psychologist who years ago worked at Bellevue hospital, stated: Out of 100 people from age 21 to age 65, 8 will wind up in a mental institution, 16 more will be profoundly neurotic, 16 more will be deeply neurotic, and 16 more will be mildly neurotic. That's more than half, so perhaps sometimes when we're dealing with people on a daily basis they look normal to us but some of them have real stuff going on inside.

So essentially, the vast majority of us are "functional neurotics." We all have our hang-ups and our preconceived notions and they are not always based on reality. They are based on our perception of reality or our "map" and sometimes our maps are wrong. That's why a lot of people are going to counseling and they are seeking out help. They want to find more efficient, better, more effective methods for coping with life on a daily basis. The normal state is BLISS and a lot of us don't have it. A lot of us don't have joy in our lives on a daily basis when in fact that is our given.

Take, for example, a little baby. What do they require for happiness? Couple of meals a day and a place to sleep? Children make up games as they go along. "Bang! You're dead. Now get back up and be a new guy!" Totally unrestricted and they are joyful and then we shove stuff on them, on top of them saying, "Shouldn't do this. You can't do this. Don't do that. You must do this." Eventually they throw up their hands because they don't know how to react.

People are said to have nervous breakdowns. No nerves break down. You can't show me a broken nerve on a nervous breakdown. No one is born insane. It's hard to realize that some people choose that form of behavior as a means for putting responsibility for taking care of themselves on someone else. That's why I'm so concerned with teaching responsibility.

I want to be response-able in any situation. I can't control what happens to me although there are philosophers and metaphysics people who say we bring it on ourselves because we have to learn that lesson. However I can still choose how I REACT.

Let's assume that that is only partially correct. Viktor Frankl, in a concentration camp, said the one thing he vowed was that he was not going to let them take away how he would choose to react to what happened. No matter what took place he was going to survive and was going to get out and write a book and teach people so that this could never happen again. That's what kept him alive through the death camps. He crawled out between dead bodies stark naked in the middle of winter.

So if he could choose how to react under those conditions then surely we can choose how to react with snow on the ground, or if it's cold outside, or whatever our major catastrophic problems are. That's the idea of getting the tools to maintain some semblance of control as to how we react in any situation, including relationships.

Using the goal setting techniques described earlier, we can build wonderful relationships at home, at work, and at play. An excellent text for getting clear on our romantic relationships is the book by Barbara DeAngelis, Are You the One For Me?[*] I buy these in bulk and give copies to many of my young adult patients who are searching for a "significant other" as their partner.

I mentioned earlier in this chapter about the importance of good relationships in the place where you work and that a bad work environment can actually kill you or at the very least, critically impair your health. Here is an experiment you can try yourself so you will see just how real the challenge is.

---

[*] see references

1. Do your own independent survey. Write this question on a piece of paper or a three by five card and carry it with you so you can ask as many people you want until you see the proof yourself. The language is very specific.

Q: "If a man under the age of 55 or 60 years is an employee and he works five days a week, Monday through Friday, from 9-5, which day of the work week is most stressful, the one day he would most likely have a heart attack? What day would you guess?

Then pause, wait for their answer. You will see for yourself that 8 or 9 out of 10 will guess Monday! Why? It is the thought of going back to a job they dislike so intensely that it puts them at risk for a heart attack. The study concluded that there are more attacks in this age group on Monday than on Tuesday, Wednesday, Thursday, and Friday combined.

A team of psychologists surveyed many men in this age group who survived their Monday morning heart attack. They asked them, "What were you thinking about Sunday evening and/or Monday morning?" The consensus was the idea that they (sometimes in a joke) would state, "I'd rather DIE than put in one more day on a job I HATE!"

Well, the unconscious mind has difficulty differentiating from a vividly imagined experience and a real one. (Just imagine waking up from a nightmare, totally imagined but seemingly very real.) I think survival is a pretty good reason to learn how to build wonderful relationships on the job or to find a job where people work together in harmony.

The heart hears what the mind says and replies, "No problem, we'll just give you a heart attack and then

111

you do not have to go back to that job you hate." (Of course, it might kill you but at least it is a legitimate excuse for not showing up for work.) Now, we have a whole new field of medicine: Psycho-neuro immunology.

It is very important to recall that the only one you can really change is yourself. Then, others change in reaction to the changes they see taking place in you.

In every large workforce it seems that some people can get along with most of their co-workers while others have very few friends on the job. Since the "workforce" is the same people, the individuals have to assume some personal responsibility in building friendly relationships with co-workers. That is what the lessons are for, to increase your own level of fun on and off the job.

The skills are worth acquiring and they also require daily practice. They will increase the quality of your life and as in the examples stated, they might even SAVE your life, too!

Let's take another look at ROMANTIC relationships. If you are currently between engagements (that is also the show biz term for temporarily out of work) and would like to get involved with someone new, there are some excellent guidelines for improving your odds.

One method is to go back to the pen and paper and describe the characteristics of an imaginary ideal partner. What do you really want, if you could create it? Make a list as long as you can in each of the areas that are important to you. Remember, in brainstorming suspend critical judgement. We can do that later. Right now just go for quantity of ideas and characteristics.

I attended a seminar on relationships years ago, presented by a well-known female author. She brought a gentleman up on the stage and asked him to describe the physical qualities of his ideal future mate. The speaker wrote the list on a chalkboard.

Then she asked him to imagine what that female would probably want on her list for Mr. Perfect. He did what she asked. Then she said to him, "Step back, take a look at HER list and tell me how close YOU come to being that individual." Of course, he laughed and said, "NO WAY!"

Then she said, "Perhaps now you know why she is not here with you this evening." Everybody had a good laugh at this gentleman's expense. But the point was well made.

Once we design our ideal individual and finish our long dream list, then we do a reality check. We can then see if it is possible to become more like the person that our dream person would like, or we have to become a little more realistic in setting our sights.

I spend some time regularly at a local health club. It is easy to spot the newly divorced people, who for the first time in twenty years are trying to get back into better physical condition before they re-enter the dating arena. It makes you wonder if they would have stayed in better shape, would they still be married to their former partners?

Of course, physical fitness is just one area for improvement. I have found that it seems opposites may attract but similarities or common interests keep people together. Ask some people you know who have been together happily for years what keeps the fire of attraction going.

It pays to remember that you cannot really change anybody else. It is hard enough to work on yourself. Sometimes when you do change, others will change in reaction to the changes they see taking place in you. For example with couples, if both are overweight and one decides to get physically trim, very often the partner will follow. This is even more likely to occur if they start by walking together a few times a week. This is just one example.

In the dating scene, it is actually easier to find someone with similar hobbies and interests by joining and getting active in selected groups. If you really enjoy skiing, join your nearest ski club and get on the committee. Go on the ski trips and meet other singles who also like to ski.

If you like tennis, join a tennis club and take some lessons. Join the mixed leagues. The same is true for any sport or activity you enjoy. It is much easier to find someone who actually enjoys what you enjoy rather than trying to convert somebody later. Whether it is visiting the art museum, volunteering to help the local symphony or theater, attending or teaching adult education classes at the local colleges or high schools, the choices are unlimited.

The same is true with religious or spiritual group affiliations. By getting active, you meet others with similar interests. It is much more fun to be with people who like the same things you do. The relationship chemistry has a better chance under these favorable circumstances.

I already mentioned Barbara DeAngelis's book <u>Are You the One for Me?</u> Another great book on the same subject is by Reverend Joan Gattuso, titled <u>A Course in</u>

<u>Love</u>*, which emphasizes the spiritual view on relationships.

Life is much more fun when you can share your experiences with a significant other. However, the best relationships are based on inter-dependent people who do not NEED another person to feel whole or complete. They choose a companion to share life experiences. People who think they need another person to be whole tend to enter into co-dependent relationships.

The question is: Do you want to be needed (which gets heavy after a while) or do you desire to be WANTED by someone who is with you by choice, to share the good times and the occasional challenges we all face from time to time? You have a choice.

CHAPTER 9

Setting & Getting Goals

Earlier, I mentioned the importance of goals, including the Yale study completed more than thirty years ago. I thought that once this information was published, every upper level schoolteacher would be imparting this knowledge to each and every student. I thought that every parent, capable of reading, would reinforce these concepts at home. I was wrong.

I recently attended a marvelous lecture by Brian Tracy in greater Cleveland, at the Peak Performers Network meeting, and saw more than 800 attendees, most with above average intelligence and many who were eager to improve their own lifestyles, sitting and taking notes like crazy, not wanting to let even one good idea escape.

Mr. Tracy, to prove a point, asked the same question from the Yale University study, about how many had written goals on their person that evening. Because of the mix of this particular group, the number was about 10%, two or three times the national average of college students.

Tracy tried to make light of the sad observation, and then went on to repeat Nightingale's information of the Strangest Secret. He stated that even today, more than forty years after Earl Nightingale assembled his statistics (see Chapter 1) the numbers are STILL about the same!

Once you finish this book and develop your own personal plan of action, perhaps we can start the movement to help others and thereby increase the quality of life for all that will follow the collective examples.

Part of the sad truth is that the vast majority of schoolteachers spend a lot of time on study plans and students' homework assignments and some continuing education for their careers and licensing or certification. But the commonly held belief is that the system will take care of our futures, so we do not need to set a lot of personal goals. Even those pursuing their masters degree or Ph.D. who already have their goals firmly set in their minds, often succumb to the belief that the system will somehow take control and guide them toward their best futures.

If you have school age children, the next time you have a parent-teacher meeting do your own survey. Ask your child's teacher, "Do you carry on your person a list of your own personal goals?" Let me know what you discover. Nightingale said the average was 5%. If the teachers do not practice this, instilling it in your children becomes YOUR responsibility, once you do it for yourself. First, what you DO is infinitely more important than what you say or tell your children to do. Nothing works better than your example. Do YOURS first, then assist them in assembling their own book of dreams and goals. It can be a lot of fun and have significance beyond your wildest dreams.

Many years ago I taught my oldest son, around his tenth year, all about aviation and model airplanes. Years later, when he saw me get a private pilot's license, an instrument rating and then the materialization of the exact airplane from my goal book to our local airport and in my aircraft hangar, he went out and got his own license and soon after, his own airplane, too. We share the love of aviation as father and son. What you do means a lot more than what you say.

By now, you are more fully aware of the importance of setting goals. Is it possible to have a good life without goals? There are philosophers who will tell you that it is possible to be spontaneous, to stay "in the present moment" but the two are not mutually exclusive. Part of the Buddhist philosophy says, "Get clear on the desired outcome (set your goal), detach yourself from the outcome and become part of the PROCESS."

When I first heard this it seemed confusing to me. I asked a friend of mine who was more familiar with this school of thought to give me an example in language I might be better able to understand. He explained:

> Suppose that we are in Cleveland, Ohio and we decide to drive to New York City to attend an Eyecare Convention Weekend. We call the auto club and request some maps for the trip. We call one of the convention hotels and secure our room reservations. We get the convention brochures and register on the Internet for the classes we want to attend.
>
> But after all of this, we are still in Cleveland, Ohio. Our next step is to "detach" from the desired outcome of "New York City" and get into the car and start the actual "journey," by driving east.
>
> We do stay in the present moment, and enjoy the scenery and the progress along the desired route. We stop along the way for some great food and then continue on our journey towards our destination. The drive requires our full attention at the legal speed to enjoy a great trip.

The same principles apply for almost any goals we want. We get "clear" on the desired outcome. We do the necessary preparation. Then, we begin the journey in the direction of our dreams. We enjoy every step along the way.

One of the methods for setting goals includes a timetable, the time by when the goal will be realized. A goal without a deadline is just a wish. We need to know "a time by when the goal will be realized."

The only exceptions are altered behaviors, which we can reach and then continue to maintain. We use a timetable or schedule to get there and behavior modification to stay there.

Earlier I mentioned my former weight problem. Once I recognized the danger to my health, I set a timetable to attain my ideal weight. When I reached the "goal" I set a new goal of maintaining the same weight and I check it once a week. Years have passed since the original goal was set, but I am still on the course of maintaining good health. For this type of goal, first you attain, and then you maintain the results. So, what goals do you want to reach?

Let's review 6 of the 7 most important areas of our lives that we have discussed so far, the chapters three through eight.

In chapter 3, Determining Your Desired Outcome(s), there was an emphasis on YOUR. So often we spend our lives helping others reach their goals and we forget about our own. It is possible to do both as long as you stay focused. We do live in an interdependent society and reaching our goals involves helping others fill their needs, too. Just remember to develop the win-win philosophy (I win and you win too, versus the I win and you lose concepts).

Start by writing your desired outcome(s) in your journal. Review chapter 3 and begin the fun process. By using a loose-leaf binder with dividers and tabs we can list our major goals in each important category.

In chapter 4, the KNOWING section, we brought into focus that we are indeed in the INFORMATION AGE. A century ago it required a lot of work to acquire knowledge. Today you can uncover or discover anything you want if you have access to a public library or a computer and the Internet.

Reading non-fiction as little as fifteen to thirty minutes a day can make a big difference in your life and the lives of those around you. Anything that increases your vocabulary can also have a huge positive effect on your income and the joy of fine literature.

In your GOALS BINDER, what new things did you want to know or need to know to increase your knowledge for pleasure and to be more valuable to the "market-place"? You can get paid for what you know and for how you use that knowledge to add value.

For chapter five, the BEING section, list your desired goals for what you want to BE or become. You can become virtually anything you choose by following the guidelines and carefully selecting your role models. Reread this chapter and remember as a child being asked, "So what do you want to BE when you grow up?" Pretend you are a child and reflect on that question. Then realize that it is never too late to have a happy childhood.

People of all ages are returning to adult education classes and changing careers. Most companies are looking for self-motivated individuals who are into continuing education for life. Other individuals are turning their hobbies, their labor of love into home-based businesses. Two famous examples in, of all things, the COOKIE business, are Wally "Famous Amos" and Mrs. Fields. Their stories are legends.

While, the failure rate in new businesses is very high, the risks can be minimized by carefully selecting a role model who has already done what you want to do or something similar and acquire the necessary knowledge about owning your own business.

I have been able to analyze many business opportunities over the years and I learned how to ask a lot of questions. For example, when I interview the owner of a small business I might ask, "What do you like BEST about having your own business? What do you like LEAST about having your own business? How did you first decide to have your own business? Why did you pick this particular business? How did you select this location?" The list goes on.

Another method is to read the trade publications where franchises are offered. Send away for the free kits and see what they offer. Remember, too, that a lot of entrepreneurs have done extremely well with many major corporations by getting to know all they can about the company and increasing their own personal abilities to become more valuable.

In chapter six, the DOING chapter, remember as you develop and implement your new plans, to list what you want to DO, what you will be doing one year from now out to five years from now. By writing in your binder or journal you sharpen your focus. As you know, before you build a new house you must first develop the blueprint.

For chapter seven, GETTING AND HAVING is what most of us aspire to do so that we can enjoy nice possessions. For years I owned a fast boat and was able to teach all of my children how to water-ski. Living in Cleveland, Ohio on Lake Erie we spent a lot of Sunday afternoons in the summer out on the lake followed by picnics on the shore. Getting and having were necessary to add all of those happy memories for the photo album.

Later I learned to fly and acquired my own plane, a magic carpet and time machine combined. I even got to compete in the Labor Day weekend Cleveland Air Races three years in a row, in the Proficiency Derby. The third year I took first place and retired from racing.

Getting and Having with sharing improved the quality of my life and that of my family members. Try the storyboard or dream-board described in chapter seven. It works!

In chapter eight, Relating and Relationships, there is a lot of information available and several excellent references listed here. Of all the sources of joy, our relationships offer the greatest potential. Anyone, regardless of their past history, can learn how to increase the quality and quantity of their relationships.

When my children come to visit me, they are fascinated by all of the people we encounter who treat me like a long-time friend. For example, the gentleman who restocks our shelves at our local supermarket always has a kind word. If he sees me he always stops to converse for a minute and is eager to help me find what I am looking for. How did this happen?

From the first time I met him, while he was restocking the shelves, I stopped, introduced myself, gave him a business card and SHARED a funny story with him. I noticed that very few customers even stop to talk to him unless they need help from him. It is a lonely job in spite of the fact that he is surrounded by passing customers while he works, virtually non-stop.

By taking a few moments and telling him that my family was in the grocery business when I was growing up and commenting on how hard he works, I showed a respect that established a friendship. The last time I was there he reminded me how it is nice to get a kind word and some recognition, even from a passing stranger who he now considers a friend. I try to do this everywhere I shop or dine or bank. I get excellent, friendly service as a result.

In any new relationship someone has to take the initiative. I call these random acts of kindness. Try to be the first to GIVE in a new relationship and see what happens. Then use your journal to record what you want, what you are willing to give FIRST and then what you receive.

As you put together all the pieces you will build a phenomenal life. I like the line from Frank Sinatra's version of one of his favorite songs, "Regrets, I've had a few, but too few to mention." You too can do it your way as long as you keep in mind the definition of enlightenment: "With good for all concerned."

Author and motivational speaker Nido Qubein tells the story that when he first came to this country from Lebanon as a young man he realized the importance of learning the new language. Each day he would select 10 words, write them in a notebook, look up the definition and work to memorize those words and use them throughout the day. The next day he would learn 10 more words, follow the same procedure, and use those new words along with the previous day's words throughout his interactions.

At the end of one year he had more than two thousand words that he had added to his vocabulary; after the second year he had more words than most Americans use regularly. The average American without a college education has a WORKING VOCABULARY, what they use on a daily basis. The average American's working vocabulary consists of about four hundred words, which consist of repeated phrases such as, "you know," and "like." Profanity, when used, is thought to be used as a result of an inadequate vocabulary.

Today, Mr. Qubein is a published author, has built a major corporation and has become a multimillionaire. His command of the English language keeps him on the speaker's circuit. His message is clear. "If I can come to this country as a young man with NO English vocabulary and through regular study became an expert and financially secure for life, so can you." He acquired and utilizes the knowledge that makes it possible.

In one of Napoleon Hill's books, The Master Key to Riches, Hill lists the methods used by countless numbers of millionaires to attain fame and fortune. I previously mentioned BURNING DESIRE. You really have to be "ON FIRE" to make it happen.

For example, you have two employees you are considering to fill one opening at a higher level position. When interviewed, one says, "I'll give it my best shot." The other says, "I'll do WHATEVER it takes!" Which one would you promote?

Hill also mentions the "Master-Mind" alliance, where two or more people who are working to get ahead (but not necessarily for the same cause) emotionally support each other to follow their own dreams. Whatever endeavor is being pursued becomes much more fun and easier to do. This is not a new idea as it dates back to biblical days, "where two or more gather..."

For years Jack Boland, a Unity minister, designed and marketed MASTER MIND* journals. New books are still available for every year and provide daily inspiration as well as a place to record your thoughts and your progress. In my opinion, they are an excellent investment.

Between Hill's book and the Master Mind journal you will know what you need to do and how to do it. Remember that EFFICIENCY is doing things the right way and EFFECTIVENESS is doing the right things. You need to be clear on both.

One of the major benefits of the loose-leaf binders is that in a few minutes a day you can review each of the TOP goals in each section. It does not take long when you are organized. Remember the importance of concentrating on only ONE goal at a time for each list.

My favorite comparison is the commercial laser versus the light bulb. Both, in fact, emit light rays. The bulb may illuminate the room but the industrial laser can cut through a piece of steel. We can say, "It has its act

---

* see references

together." It is clearly focused and accelerated. Become a goal-getting laser. Get focused and get accelerated.

You want measurable progress in reasonable time. I still remember Earl Nightingale's definition of success as, "the PROGRESSIVE REALIZATION of a worthy goal or ideal." It sill makes a lot of sense.

It is worth it to re-read the previous chapters. Get very clear on your desired outcomes. Do SOMETHING every day in the direction of your goals. The early pioneers and settlers WALKED across the United States. They had a burning desire. They crossed rivers and climbed mountains. It took a long time but they made some progress every day and eventually reached their destination.

On a different scale, the Gold Medal winners of the Olympics practice for several hours five or six days a week, sometimes for three or four years, preparing for their chance to win the medal and recognition.

You can get any goal or goals you really want if you just do what others have done to achieve the same results. Get clear, get a plan, do your homework and preparation and Go For It! Positive action in the direction of your dreams mixed with daily measurable progress can bring you virtually anything you want.

It also helps us to remember daily that the best way to have our goals become reality is to help enough other people to reach their goals, fulfill their needs and to help their dreams come true.

CHAPTER 10

Putting It All Together

Because of the repeated references to "who is driving your bus?" the concept of putting it all together is like planning a fantastic vacation or a trip to a new location. You get to drive anywhere you want! By now, you have a better idea of where you have been and what is even more important, where you would like to go, starting NOW! You have new insights. You have new "tools" for change.

You have a much better idea of what is really important to you and what is not. Just like the earlier references of planning the trip, you must first get clear about where 'A' is. Some of the personal inventory lists, when written into your journal make this much easier to do.

The list of morning questions from Chapter 3 is reprinted here. See if part 'B' is a lot easier to do, now that you have finished the previous chapters.

A	B
Who am I?	Who could I be?
Where am I going?	Where could I be going?
What am I doing?	What could I be doing?
Why?	**Why?**

You now have more tools to plan the rest of your life. By assuming responsibility for how to choose your desired outcomes, how you choose what to study and know, and getting clear on 'Being, Doing, Getting and Having and Relationships,' you design the map(s) for the fantastic journey called LIFE.

It becomes easier to set goals and get goals when you have clearly defined objectives. There is a tremendous inner peace that comes when you are 'on course.'

Whether you now have a good grip on the reins of your race horse, the handle bars of your new Harley, the steering wheel of your new red Ferrari, or the helm of your new yacht, now you get to decide what direction to go and whatever destination you want.

This chapter will briefly review the previous ones, help you to use the new tools and put you back in control and keep you in control from now on. Once you incorporate these principles you will permanently remove yourself from the category of victim and finally take back control of the seven most important areas of your life.

The sense of peace is even greater when you fully realize, as I mentioned before, that enlightenment means "with good for all concerned," the win-win versus I win and they lose. People with a higher consciousness know that the "good life" comes most easily through SERVICE to others.

Even in the manufacturing and retail businesses, the leaders all acknowledge that if you find a NEED and fill it in a superior manner, ultimately all of your needs will also be met. This is their way of serving others.

I just recently attended a three-day weekend convention and got to hear Dr. Wayne Dyer and Dr. Bill Glasser. While the methods they use and the backgrounds of each are different, the approaches were very similar. Find a way or ways to serve others and find true joy.

Dr. Glasser stressed the importance of being careful when you make choices. His original text, <u>Reality Therapy</u>* and one of his newer books <u>Choice Theory</u>* demonstrate the power of choice. In a nutshell he states that we all have needs that we want to satisfy. Some of us do it in a responsible manner that works and some of us do it in an irresponsible manner, which does not work, at least not long-range. His books are worth owning and reading.

I especially appreciate that his present age at this writing is 78 years young. He is as sharp as ever. So there is hope, even for us seniors, to make a significant difference for the better in the lives of the people we impact.

Dr. Dyer has many books and tapes, all worth owning. Everyone who sees him lecture feels like a long-time friend. They line up to have him autograph the books and he gets more hugs in an hour than some people get in a year. I believe it is because he is genuinely trying and succeeding to help others with his messages. He almost missed his airplane out of Cleveland because the crowd wanted him to stay long past the scheduled end of the presentation.

Your life can also be filled with warmth and sensitivity as you apply the principles in this book, too. The key,

---

* see references

like the student in school, is measurable progress in reasonable time. You really will feel great when you do what needs to be done WHEN it needs to be done (whether you feel like doing it at that time, or not.)

We have talked about 'A,' where the next segment of the journey starts and now, let us take another look at 'B,' the first check-point on this new segment.

As we compile our lists of what brings us real happiness and joy, the 'B' becomes more clearly defined. I like to look at where I want to be, first five years out and then I work backwards to four, three, two and one.

There is an N.L.P. technique using timelines. It is a lot of fun and easy to do. Imagine walking out on your timeline or yellow brick road if you prefer, to where you could ideally be in five years. The location, the sights and sounds, the cast of characters, and the scenery are all important. Let your imagination soar.

Then take a deep breath, exhale slowly and physically look back over your shoulder, and visualize the road that got you there. Where did you come from? Where were you the year before (four years from the starting point 'A') and then three, two and one.

Once you have the pictures, close your eyes for a moment, then return back to the starting point 'A.' Pause and write down your experience. In the future you will be amazed at how right your vision was, because you will make it a reality. Remember the words to the song, "You gotta HAVE A DREAM in order to make the dream come true."

Set aside a few minutes for planning time at least five days a week. Most people find that early morning works best. Earl Nightingale told me years ago that he loved to get up about an hour before the family, maybe have just a cup of coffee and then spend that quiet time putting thoughts and ideas on paper. He built a huge career doing this.

In my earlier references to modeling excellence I stated to ask yourself who has the kind of life you want? What is different about their life? Can you use all or at least parts of their recipe?

In one of his programs Brian Tracy said, "If you steal words from one writer that is called plagiarism. If you borrow from a hundred writers, that is called research. I do A LOT of research." So do I.

Learn from others, the successes and the failures. Try new things. See what works and what does not. RESULTS are the name of the game. Richard Bandler (N.L.P.) repeats the question, "Does it work for you? Is it fair to all?" If not, DO SOMETHING ELSE!"

How many activities in your life no longer produce the desired results? Be honest. Start the process of replacing activities that no longer satisfy with things that do. So often we seem to do things that we have "always done" because we forget to ask if something else might be better.

Sometimes we have negative people in our lives at work or at play. As you grow spiritually you may have to adopt a policy of "selective abandonment" of negative influences, and replace them with more positive people.

One of my clients complained because her husband used to go out with the guys two or three nights a week to drink beer because he was so unhappy with his job. He liked to be with his fellow workers because they did not like their jobs either, so they had a lot in common, like the old saying "misery loves company."

With much coaching, she encouraged him to go to college in the evenings instead of the bar. In two years he got a degree in computers and landed a great job that he really loves. He had to abandon the bar buddies and the bar scene to make the major move. Now he socializes with a new group of fellow workers who enjoy their work. It has also tremendously benefited his home life, win-win.

Brian Tracy said two of the most important factors that impact your life are the books you read and the company you keep. By switching to a different crowd, he is now enjoying his job and his new circle of friends.

Now, you might want to make a copy of the following list and tape it to the corner of your mirror in the bedroom or bathroom to serve as a daily reminder. The SEVEN most important areas we have covered are:

I.   DETERMINING WHAT YOU DESIRE

II.   KNOWING

III.   BEING

IV.   DOING

V.   GETTING AND HAVING

VI.   RELATIONSHIPS

VII.   SETTING AND GETTING GOALS

In the beginning you may choose to ask yourself the following questions as you incorporate these ideas into your busy schedule.

1. Is what I am doing the highest and best use of my time, right now?
2. Is this part of the 20% of activities that will bring me the 80% of the results? Can I get someone else to do the other 80% that produces the lesser results?
3. Are my activities taking me closer to or farther from my listed objectives?

I firmly believe in the importance of recreation as a part of my life plan. I separate my work and my play (although much of my work is a lot of fun because I engage in a labor of love). Because I plan carefully, when I play, it is guilt-free. I do not take my briefcase to the beach or on the boat. I inform my key people ahead of time. Do not call me unless it is a national, family, or genuine emergency that cannot wait. Otherwise, save it until I return to work.

After decades in business I also know that no one on their death bed ever said, "I should have spent more time at the office." The key is BALANCE.

Invest the time to read and re-read this book more than once. Use it as a tour guide for the journey of your life. If you have friends that want to get more out of life, encourage them to get their own copy (so they can review it whenever they want) and form your own Master-Mind group. Meet on a regular basis.

Your progress will be accelerated. You can share in each other's joy. Just watch the T.V. when they zoom in on the victorious team at any sporting event. See the thrill of the shared victory. When you do, you realize that life is the best game and it is more fun when you win because with these methods, everybody can win and no one has to lose. Start now – I wish you all the best.

CHOICE

The journey of the soul begins with understanding that we are drawn automatically as a species to come to terms with power. Each human being is experiencing the causes and effects of his or her choices, his or her desires to fill in the empty, powerless places within him or her. This dynamic can be described in terms of an insecure humanity, but that is just the obvious. The mechanism at work is the journey toward genuine, authentic empowerment.

This is why each human being struggles so deeply with power: the lack of it, the acquisition of it, what it is really, how one should have it. Underlying every crisis, emotional, spiritual, physical and psychological, is the issue of power. Depending upon the lens that you wear to interpret your crisis, you will either step closer to your soul or closer to the Earth.

The journey to wholeness requires that you look honestly, openly and with courage into yourself, into the dynamics that lie behind what you feel, what you perceive, what you value, and how you act. It is a journey through your defenses and beyond so that you can experience consciously the nature of your personality, face what it has produced in your life, and choose to change that.

-      Gary Zukav

Reprinted with the permission of
Simon and Schuster Adult Publishing Group
From THE SEAT OF THE SOUL by Gary Zukav
Copyright 1989 by Gary Zukav

REFERENCES

1. "The Strangest Secret"

   Earl Nightingale

   Nightingale-Conant Co. 1-800-525-9000

   6245 W. Howard St. Niles, IL 60714

2. PsychoCybernetics

   Dr. Maxwell Maltz & Dan Kennedy

   Also Nightingale-Conant Co.

3. In Search of Excellence

   Tom Peters and Robert Waterman

   Harper Collins, November 1982

4. Finding Flow

   Mihaly Csikszentmihali

   Publisher: Basic Books, April 1998

5. "Self Actualization"

   Abraham Maslow

   Audiocassette, Publisher: Soundworks; (1985)

6. Rich Dad, Poor Dad

   Robert Kiyosaki & Sharon L. Lechter

   Publisher: Warner Books, April 1, 2000

7. Attracting Romance

   Lowell Jay Arthur

   Publisher: Distinctive Publishing Co. 1992

8. "Success Mastery Academy"

   Brian Tracy

   Audiocassettes: Nightingale-Conant Co.

9. "How To Have Your Best Year Ever!"

   Jim Rohn

Videotape series: Jim Rohn International

10. The Celestine Prophecy

James Redfield

Publisher: Warner Books, 1993

11. Alice in Wonderland

Lewis Carroll

12. Laws of Success & Think and Grow Rich & The Master Key to Riches

Napoleon Hill

Publisher: Random House

The Ballantine Publishing Group: 1-800-733-3000

13. Beware of the Naked Man Who Offers You His Shirt & How to Swim With the Sharks

Harvey Mackay

Publisher: Ivy Books – Ballantine Books 1990

Publisher: Morrow, 1988

14. Core Transformation

Connirae and Tamara Andreas

Publisher: Real People Press, November, 1996

15. The Artist's Way

Julia Cameron

Publisher: J.P. Tarcher, February 2002

16. Games People Play

Eric Berne

Publisher: Ballantine Books, reissue: August 1996

17. I'm O.K., You're O.K.

Thomas Harris

Publisher: Avon, reissue: September 1996

18. General Semantics

Alfred Korzybski

Publisher: Institute of General Semantics, 2nd ed.:June 1997

19. Are You the One for Me?

Barbara DeAngeles

Publisher: Island Books, reprint ed. June 1993

20. A Course in Love

Reverend Joan Gattusso

Publisher: Harper, February 1997

21. The Grapes of Wrath

John Steinbeck

Publisher: Penguin USA roughcut ed. January 2002

22. "Master Mind Journals"

Jack Boland

Publisher: Master Mind Publisher, June 1992

Renaissance Unity

P.O. Box 280

Warren, Michigan 48090-0280

23. Reality Therapy & Choice Theory

Dr. William Glasser

Publisher: Perennial, reissue: November 1989, Feb 1999

24. Manifest Your Destiny

"The Secrets to Manifesting Your Destiny" cassettes

Wayne Dyer

Publisher: Nightingale-Conant Co.

25. "The Seat of the Soul"

Gary Zukov

Publisher: Simon and Shuster

ABOUT THE AUTHOR

Dr. Erwin Jay, O.D.

Erwin Jay is a professional speaker, author, Certified Master Practitioner of Neuro-Linguistic Programming, practice management consultant, seminar leader, and optometrist. His articles have been published in every major journal in the eyecare profession and he has lectured extensively to sales and service organizations.

His own multi-office, multi-doctor group practice compelled him to become knowledgeable about the business aspects of professions. Several years ago, this expertise led to his appointment as a divisional vice-president of a major publicly held corporation, (NYSE listed) a position he held for three years.

Throughout his professional and business careers he has had an unending quest for understanding how and why successful people achieve such outstanding results that are many times greater than the averages. This pursuit led him to the field of NLP, which shows how our brains really work, what separates the great from the not-so-great and how these skills can be learned by anyone with the desire. He conducts NLP training classes for companies and organizations on improving the effectiveness of communications, self-motivation and results-orientation.

In addition to his busy work schedule, he is an instrument-rated pilot, an Aviation Safety Counselor for the Federal Aviation Authority, a speaker at Aviation Safety Seminars and a former air-race competitor. His hobbies include aviation, skiing, and world travel.

Dr. Jay has the ability to help individual companies and organizations develop fresh ways of solving problems by increasing the ability to clearly define their objectives and improving the necessary communications skills that build a more cohesive team-oriented approach.

You can contact the author at:

Email askdrjay@bigplanet.com

Or call (440) 446-1236

CPSIA information can be obtained
at www.ICGtesting.com
Printed in the USA
FFOW05n0646261214